The Ronin Poetz is an excerpt of the ever expanding volumes Ancient-Art-of-Facts Vol I. Copyright © 2000

DaChosen PUBLISHING

Printed in the Untied States of America

ISBN# 0-9762627-1-1

Acknowledgments

This book is dedicated to Tracey Wingfield for her devotion to this project and all her sacrifices

Ray Cosico for his cover artwork I also give thanx to Phillip A. King for his artwork, although not featured

Thanx to my parents, Willis Thomas III (Father Aquarius) and Deloris Thomas (Mother Pisces) To my brothers Bryan (strong) and Jason (hero)

Thanx to the 3 allies, jamaal, sha-nun, and rufus Other allies include Quyionah Wingfield, Jehvon Buckner, Dr. Suzar Epps, Christopher Russel, Brother Shabazz, Bro. Razw.e.l., Blackdot, Bro. Chris, Kofi Candela, Jamel Robinson, Walter Geer, Knowledge, Mona Webb (and the Poetry Alliance)

and the remaining friends, allies, teachers, and enemies, (thank u)

The Ronin Poetz

By

Teferu Azr

TABLE OF CONTENTS

Act III: Take a Right 2 Passage

The Prologue

"the song of swordz"
        by Father Aquarius

251-ST
file # of the enemy
pale king's mark
tyrannical ruler of huemanity --- crab like, cancerous
slanderous pictures of Death
nailed in the alleyways of war torn cities
these posters of the impostor represent The Pale King
but no one knows who,
or what,
lies behind the veil of secrecy
be it one diabolical man
or an entire governing body

my ink runs water
pen speaking silently
i hide in the shadows of syllables
because my commentary
can be retaliated against
violently
4 those already taken

The Prologue: The Song of Swordz

my pen taps their voices and bleeds them
speaking of this pale king's tyranny
he is the insidious, clever, clandestine puppet master
who brought an end 2 illusionary freedom

many awoke in the wake
of the pale king's dictator-ship
flying
abusive banners
binding the world
by buying the world with lies and a smile
subtly seducing
from a kingdom named MUSA, false civilizer of nations
war and a burning cross as his secret oath
            and sign-ing on the dotted, descendant
of an unholy bloodline
while kindly colonizing,
parading and prancing the lands as a gentle benefactor
orchestrating wars
and marching a million orwellian soldiers
thought holders, thought police
from the mind, 2 the body, 2 the soul
2 the convolutions of the earth
and the veins pumping people in2 the roads and streets

march! march! came their beat
re-wiring reality and language
the earth lay in anguish
pale king held mother down
while pumping pressure,
penetrating
and desecrating sacred grounds
volcanoes
hurricanes mixed with tornadoes
and earthquakes
make the sounds
of mother earth 2 scream
while her elements were enslaved 2 run machines
that ran all over her,
polluting mother's air, fire, earth, and water

The Prologue: The Song of Swordz

machines hold mother earth down
making her go blind
the original people stood by
seduced by the illusions and the lies
letting mother earth die
the pale king's laughter
bathing in her coal
stressing her alchemical tithe
diamonds were the tears she cried

and how could we 4get
the pale king's experiments
his search 4 life in2 the succulent messiah sequence
of the genetics of melanin,
the 2nd burning of the Khemetic Libraries
he searched 2 break the code
2 encode the spiritual flow
that lay buried inside us
pumping pineal fluids and the blood of moorish druids
in2 a still body that waits 4 u 2 lie still
as the pale king still lies 2 u that he is a precious lover
jacob's tricknological hunter
the daughter of morality's grafted brother
he commits incest
this pale king infects the minds of slain warriors
their bodies outlined in his design
his heartbeat iz another black warrior's flatline
talk 2 the bloodline --- written script of The Book of Life
our blood types rhythm (rah's hymn) --- preach deliberate
this still liar needs your blood 2 function
and now, black babies' tears r the 1st things that spill from
the womb
water broken tombs
diluted black babies hanging from flagpoles
swinging rag dolls at the angle of 33 degrees
the boiling point of tricknology
black blood, fine wine, melanin colt .45, 85% proof
only 5% r in the loop
recycled warriors
spilt blood, bleeding lips

<u>The Prologue: The Song of Swordz</u>

i speak as a bloody orator
as hope feeds off the fruit of my family tree
while still breathing thru a respirator
speaking sharpened light
as our aura-tore thru the pale king's illusion
but his swift and sway, maneuvering 2wards his prey
coordinating wars in2 black lands
2 hold the Book of Life in his hands,
tightening his grip on the world

can we truly call it hypocrisy
if there was never really meant 2 be
freedom or democracy?
did we just choose 2 believe
2 get us out of the responsibility
did we just bury the hostility
that we knew this pale king's tyranny
was occupying other lands in the name of freedom
could we not taste, hear, touch, smell or see
mother earth's plea
could our own senses we not trust
as we witnessed that one kingdom was not enough
4 the pale king's insatiable lust
2 control all of nature's original sources, including us

the gluttonous malefactor's shroud had fallen
from thought, 2 pen, 2 paper
earlier the Black Warriors warned
greed had always adorned this pale king's brow
from stanzas
2 prose
but it was the pale king who had 2 make people believe
in his land of 'make believe u r free'
in order,
in this new world order
4 DEMON-acracy 2 b exposed

homeland security made sure my homeland was never secure
the pale king's armies
were making a clear and plain statement

<u>The Prologue: The Song of Swordz</u>

"all u brown skinned niggaz hit the pavement
we rounded u up and puttin' you in camps of concentration
check the fine print on that Emancipation
the proclamation was just a temporary vacation
2 your enslavement."

they killing the melanin that they lack
they're starting with the brown skinned niggaz
and working their way back
2 the true original Black

this is terrorism
not the lines in this poem
a warning,
a threat 2 him
now realize, breakdown the word 'terrorism'
and u get terra-ore
that's what the pale king has declared war for
terra means Earth
ore iz its precious substance
and all the original melanin children of the sun
rounded up in great abundance

this war will come 2 kill u
precious daughter
and precious son
this war 4 Terra-Ore
is a war 2 make sure
u never come 2gether as a people --- as ONE ...

The Prologue: Weeping Wandz

"weeping wandz"
        by Mother Pisces

t-18-1-t-15-R
file #
of this african warrior
griot,
Seth Mwindo
he added sunshine
in these dark times --- these blurry days
seth's early age
was abandoned by his mother
and raised by his father (Teihu)
who slipped thru life driven by an alcoholic haze

in drunken stirs
the father would beat
and curse
seth and his brother riso
until this single profane verse
lit a propane dirge

The Prologue: Weeping Wandz

singing the chorus of hatred
crucified at conception,
the raising
and resurrection of this black child
in2 being a True-Hue-Black Man, was now tainted

teihu would scream at his children,
"u turned your mother in2 a whore!
and u've taken my honor and sword. this honorable warrior,
guardian of my wife's garden. now unholy court-ships
fly
my wife
stolen by the moon's light.
she only glows with the faint reflection of her sons."

4 twelve years
flowed countless tears
pumped by the father's hands
until seth and his brother fled
and were nurtured by their mother's clan
9 years mastered and trained
the griot arts now pumped their veins
jogging thru the convolutions of the brain
2 exercise the knowledge of the pale king,
his thought police
and the traitorous Shogun-Aruh

when scouting 4 thought police, in troops
seth confronted the shogun
and a greater battle ensued
nature was consumed
forests became bare of trees
lush lands melted in2 deserts
and even the air could barely breathe

neither warrior could paint victory
and so their dance ended in a draw
seth felt nurtured
in the fire-arms

The Prologue: Weeping Wandz

of this enemy
bitter thoughts of battle
were sweetened by the shogun's memory
swirling in thoughts
while seth rested, unconscious
scenery changing around him

the stagehand
that opened the curtain 4 this new act
use
2
abuse
seth
he was rescued
by his father teihu
and home never looked more like heaven
where hell had been raised
and 21 years of fiery anger
sitting at the lower regions of seth
had gained enlightenment under the wings of the father
and this warrior's rage had come out of hiding ...

seth:
"i must b mistaken.
u r the aged representation
of a man who scratched his children,
pushed his wife in2 concubine, pale king service,
and dipped tongue tip
to rub bottled liquor kiss
and let free genie-alcoholic spirits
2 grant a drunkards wish."

teihu:
"my sun, my king
black hueman becoming
and warrior being,
i as the family tree still needed 2 grow
choked by the smoke of weed
and the alcoholic flow.
my lessons were the 1st 2 go,

The Prologue: Weeping Wandz

followed by my pride,
self love, and all else swallowed.
this hallucinogenic, illusionary fetish
fed me 2 sleep in the pale king's dream.
i understand your anger,
but never lose the love 4 the red, black, and green.

better 2 battle this pale notorious
than 2 keep our swords aimed only at us.
we r moors
black always gaining and building
33 degrees never enough
and if no love exists between a-moor
then what can we trust?"

cool words
mixed with
streaming tears
made up
4
twelve
dying years
the repent was genuine
and father and son
were as one

seth could see
the obscenity of his father
was now clean
the warrior black man
looked as if he could
handle a sword again

seth:
"aunt and grandmother
raised us well.
riso is a great warrior."

teihu:
"i am a ghost 2 them.

The Prologue: Weeping Wandz

u did not see me.
understand?
4 my failing 2 protect her daughter
i have slipped from her eyes
as a black man.
i warrior, up rooted
4 being abusive,
my punishment,
nothing less than being executed.

now, my son ... let me prepare 4 u
a lesson,
that will help u defeat
the shogun."

the lesson begun
2 days passed, seth returned 2 his clan
stronger ... and waiting 2 battle again

but the fight was always in his dreams
2 ask the shogun the reason
4 siding with the pale king's lies
seth's grandmother would tell him,
"the first diabolical weapon in control of the pale king
is his twisted words ... his tainted language."

seth's hunt 4 the answer became an obsession
as he himself became a myth, a legend
the syllables of his name breaking
            --- in the shaking mouths of his enemies, the thought
police
2 see this warrior's shadow
was 2 know
death
this warrior-priest quickly blessed his enemies
tactical movement
analytical supreme math
until the day his calculations brought him face-2-face
with the shogun's mask ... this 2nd clash of the titans

their powers swirled and brightened the skies
nature closed its eyes and the stars cried
2 see these 2 black bodies on opposing sides
and again,
the power of the shogun was warming
nurturing
seth quickly noticed, in their first clash
the shogun was holding back
and so it seemed
that even when he executed his father's move
it was blocked
and seth was forced 2 his knees
the griot was exhausted and admitted defeat
but he had one last plea ... "answer me this question.
what makes u serve this demon? this pale king?"

shogun-aruh:
"i tried your way once.
and it failed both me and my people.
resistance 2 the pale king brings misery and death,
my son ... seth ...
the real liars 2 reality (ruled by the pale king)
are those who have taught u 2 battle him.
they are hypocrites and confused.
they cannot even re-evolve, re-evolute.
the pale king is the ultimate truth."

and the shogun's mask was removed
and there stood the truth
seth's mother ... was shogun-aruh

shogun-aruh:
"i'll let you live, my son, and let you choose."

and the cat was killed, curious
and seth, his anger phoenixed, was now furious
he returned 2 his clan
his weapon in hand
threatening
they had kept this in4mation from him

The Prologue: Weeping Wandz

aunt and grandmother just instructed,
"kill her. she's no longer your mother.
and your father as well. we know u've seen him.
great warrior was he,
but he let your mother die spiritually
he failed as a black man. she failed as a black woman.
their judgment, is death."

their was no com4t from his brother, riso
who told him the same. "stay upon your destiny.
just because they lost their way
doesn't mean u have 2."

but seth was confused
and he returned 2 his father,
feeling more abused
            by the detainment
            of this truth
and the two met
in a field
spotlighted by the moon
and their came riso
followed by mother-aruh
and the family tree shook and withered
the battle from within

seth's mind slipped
360 degrees
reduced 2 33
burning like the leaves of his family tree
his sword
cut and killed
mother
father
and brother ... and his anger set him free
in2 a life of slavery, new found powers of tricknology
he took his mother's clothes
her shogun robes ... but the mask he left
4 the betrayal was etched on his face
4 all 2 see

The Prologue: Weeping Wandz

and the thought police
who were once his enemies
now trembled with his command
as he returned 2 his former clan
and killed them all with a gun in hand

seth was escorted back 2 the pale king ...
not as an enemy or prisoner ... but a soldier ...
heir 2 his mother's twisted crown
seth's knee bent
and he bowed down 2 his new lord and master

seth was ordained with the stain
of a new family name ... the shogun-owl
and granted a wife named Magikkk

(unbeknownst 2 the shogun,
magikkk was his half sister
born from the twisted union
of the pale king and his mother)

the shogun's natural hair burned
from mind 2 body, lost of soul
came the scars of past lashes
his jaw broken,
and 4ever unable 2 speak
the eloquent rhythms of language

the story of the weeping wands
are my inspiration
2 nurture and love
my
own
children
from the day of their conception
2 when i actually gave birth 2 them

i am mother pisces
and my children will know me
the nurturer of their trinity

The Prologue: Weeping Wandz

and they will never fight me
and grow strong
will our family tree
2 battle the pale king,
and all our culture's enemies ...

The Prologue: Word of Scoutz

"word of scoutz (no rhythm)"

FILE #888-666

"YOU ARE FREE TO DO AS WE TELL YOU ...

we are an army at the command of the Pale King.
ruthless, we spare no one
whose thoughts rest against the Pale King's desires.
no one knows what lies behind the masks of our soldiers,
except for the lies themselves
masonic in our own thought,
we soldiers of the Thought Police have abandoned individuality
for loyalty
as of now we are an army for a Police State
for the mind,
body,
soul and all the lands of the world

YOU ARE FREE TO DO AS WE TELL YOU ...

The Prologue: Word of Scoutz

with no other orders than to police and seduce thoughts,
this army,
an extension of The Pale King's might,
was once ignorantly referred to the foolish masses as The
Just
The Pale King was able to seduce the world
through the Thought Police's power of Hellywood,
tell-a-lie-vision,
sorcery Screens,
YessaBossaMassa Media,
and eMpT.V.

YOU ARE FREE TO DO AS WE TELL YOU ...

covert in our art, we Thought Police,
under the orders of The Pale King, stage horrific events that
scare
the masses into looking towards the Pale King for refuge and
security
it was us who allowed The Pale King to control wars from both
sides
often times, wars would be fought
with having one set of Thought Police battle another set
the victorious, openly working for The Pale King and crowned
as heroes,
and the vanquished (blood sacrificed) plagued and slandered
as villains.

YOU ARE FREE TO DO AS WE TELL YOU ...

the thousand headed ass of the masses bought the
deception
and slowly, we were able to march in
and claim the land under Marshal Law of the Pale King himself

YOU ARE FREE TO DO AS WE TELL YOU ...

Now, after most of the world's conquest,

The Prologue: Word of Scoutz

we reveal our true intentions
we maintain the New Order by eradicating all rebellious
thoughts against The Pale King
mainly, African Griots, Black Poets, Black Revolutionaries,
Black Writers,
all declared threats of the New Order (as well as their allies).

YOU ARE FREE TO DO AS WE TELL YOU ...

the Thought Police's most powerful technique is to fire
improper propaganda,
relying heavily on character assassination
to seduce the masses into believing their heroes are their
villains
we also specialize in the "creation" of villains, setting up
terrorist sponsored states around the world

YOU ARE FREE TO DO AS WE TELL YOU ...

before we infiltrate lands with our physical strengths,
and destructive technology,
we Thought Police first colonize the mind.

YOU ARE FREE TO DO AS WE TELL YOU ...

after placing fear into the hearts of 85% of the masses and
seducing the 10% rulers,
the 5% that remain,
will only succumb to a physical eradication
teamed with this vicious manner, there is no stopping our
army.

YOU ARE FREE TO DO AS WE TELL YOU ...

as such, we, The Thought Police, would like to commend those
of the Messiah Race
who speak ill words on others of the Messiah Race

The Prologue: Word of Scoutz

seeing the Messiah Race at each other's throats gives us insight

that our efforts in serving The Pale King are truly rewarded.

YOU ARE FREE TO DO AS WE TELL YOU ...

our guns, spells, and propaganda allow us to exploit the petty prejudices of huemans,

YOU ARE FREE TO DO AS WE TELL YOU ...

even the 'conscious' amongst you are but shades of your former existence
and their greatest sin is being too proud and self-absorbed by what they believe is knowledge;
and even they battle over the scraps that The Pale King throws to them

YOU ARE FREE TO DO AS WE TELL YOU ...

Play on ...

YOU ARE FREE TO DO AS WE TELL YOU ...

YOU ARE FREE TO DO AS WE TELL YOU ...

YOU ARE FREE TO DO AS WE TELL YOU ...

YOU ARE FREE TO DO AS WE TELL YOU ...

YOU ARE FREE TO DO AS WE TELL YOU ...

The Prologue: Cup of Warrior Juice

"cup of warrior juice"

warriors by the handful
slandered as vandals
were conscious 2 the pale king's plans

outcasted
by the very masses
they wished 2 warn
learning the secrets of their ancients
they adorned themselves
in the original knowledge
becoming Af-Ra-Kamau Griots
in these final hours
stirring up ancestral powers

The Ronin Poetz, enemies to the pale king.

unfortunately,
they had played right into this tyrant's schemes
now,
with a group of spiritually glowing black beings,
the pale king had a sequestered and outcasted team
of Original men and Original women
brightly glowing,
self actualized 2 the ancient power within them

and with a seduced Griot at his side,
it was only time that would tell if the pale king would enslave
these Warrior-Griots
and read a complete volume of their collective genetic Book of
Life.

or ... perhaps ... be defeated by The Ronin Poetz ...
ending his strife and disaster ...

welcome 2 the story of THE RONIN POETZ:
they who serve no master"

Act I: Parental Guidance

"birth in2 a nation"

i am maa kheru
the voice of truth
true of voice
being born was God's choice
my spirit unable 2 spin in time, frozen
but thru mother pisces and father aquarius, i was chozen

as it were,
i was born on the spot
where lightning, thunder, and sunbeams shock
at a time not calculated on a clock
but inbetween my mother's tear drops
my birth caused time 2 stop

but my father took the tick and tock
-- where i was born between my mother's tears --
he compounded 1 seventy-second part of each day
and created the complete year
he made the hourglass flow from bottom 2 top
my hair grew and locked

-- my father called it culture --

the pale king called it a 'cult'
and made it impure
thru his laws i was feared
my birth disturbed his unnatural order
my queen was raped when the pale king souled her
my culture's tongue was severed
but i mastered the master's language 2 mend it back 2gether
spread wordz like weather,
this morning son reign 4ever -- omega supreme
and i bring u balance when my wordz beam
sent not thru satellite but smoked signals in candlelight
1 every hour -- every 1 hour near me

i know now the conspiracy iz no theory
let me speak up -- speak proper -- speak clearly

so the pale king and his thought police can truely fear me
my people, i am here 4 thee
u can find my birth on page 3 of a new history
my speech makes up a new dictionary
it defines a clan whose styles vary ---
inebriate u like dreamberries

actually,
make u think 4 yourself (if 4 nothing else)
some of us sacrifice -- caught by the Thought Cops
we spread the sun's warmth thru city blocks
scribe hope in cement and rocks
grow new wordz as crops -- collect our props
deliver inspiration 2 the have-nots
on earth's
cursed,
knowledge-barren lot
where my culture iz hunted by cops
-- with pen and sword -- this injustice will stop
my father has given me power 2 revise the plot

chapter-by-chapter,
the truth sought and captured
caught up in the rapture
the whirlwind that b my pen
-- expression -- spoken by mouth
i shout quietly in the cup that b my paper,
i give my wordz out,
flow like water,
and like rain, drop
on this spot, where i was born

"mother pisces"

black queens sing in tune with tears
time hears their pains
and prays 2 nature 4 rain
wash them of shame,
let it drip down and b claimed by mother nature
be4 it takes her black queen away
mother earth say, "pray. shine like every ray."
cuz when light eclipses the night and shines bright
off of the sun and moon
in your womb, 3 bring raw rhythm and BOOM!

this iz a story
our mother would tell us
at night in our room

she said,
"can u sing the key of C-sons
play reasons 4 nature's waves?
the dream's won in the sun's rays
yes, sons
that's how u came in2 existence
your father pulled me up 2 him
like the attraction of water 2 the moon's call
our love was free-4-all, a free fall
and i rubbed my belly and saw a future 4 u all

i was feeling summer's heat,
responding 2 the spring air
there in your father's lips that i kissed
and he planted his two lips in my garden
i begged every part of him would resurrect in me
harmonizing with the beauty of my seed
your mother pisces,
this queen,
gave birth 2 a trinity
3 by III by three
strength, hero, justice
and my 1 wish was given 2 me

(from each of your father's eyes)

i held each of u
9 months in my womb
then i held your body anew
-- in my arms tightly -- like aset held heru
i gave u half of the personality that makes u
takes u beyond the boundaries this world made 4 u
the boundaries that try and negate u

u see, i did more than just raise u

i bathed u in the sea of wordz
taught u how 2 read and write
so your thoughts could b heard

heard in every victory song u sing
your mother,
this queen,
b the power in the thrust in your sword swing

bring u face-2-face with the gift inside u
and help u unwrap it
perfect it when u practice
help u apply it 2 your father's 4 lessons
so u can make your impression in this world
and on this journey
-- with any of life's tests -- i will b there 2 protect
until my last breath of life

and when u find my spirit filtering
in the breath of another black queen's lyrics
make that black queen your wife."

that's what my mother would tell us
in our room --- late at night

"father aquarius iii"

father aquarius scribe:
"my 3rd son, my 3rd vibe
i watch u with all 3 i's
let your brothers strength and hero guide u
when i am no longer by u
but i'll ride thru the air
share my knowledge founded by our ancestors

they who were rounded up,
not rounded off

so they r 1 stronger

able 2 bless u -- rest in u --
they r a force that wanders time
they can b channeled thru body,
soul,
and mind

so tune in

at this early age,
u r but a page 4 me 2 fill with these lessons
jailed without sentence,
my 3rd apprentice of wand,
the word,
the sword,
and the cup
that cup that will runneth over
when u r older
and the Earth gives birth 2 your queen

molds her so u can hold her,
so she can hold u and become your soldier
your truth, your friend, your lover
your children's mother
resurrect 1 another in your children's eyes
-- their voices -- your songs -- your chorus -- your vibes --

and u will teach them all that i scribe 4 u
our culture's truth
the weapon 2 battle on babylon 4 us africans

control-thought troops deserve no truce
they seduce with noose around our necks
and our culture maybe the 1st 2 die
but it iz the 1st 2 resurrect

u r the new generation
and u hold inside u the next,
formed by your queen's thoughts and breath
let me hand u wand, fill your cup, shape your sword,
and preach the word that will keep u from being sentenced
so -- my son --
let me teach -- un2 u --
these 4 lessons."

"lesson 1: the word"

"there iz no good word until u scribe it 1st,"

> lesson 1
> from Father Aquarius
> 2 his 3rd born son

"wordz come in2 existence
1st by visions that r a resistance 2 insanity."

> and trust me,
> every time i tried 2 hide from the pen it just ran 2 me
> looking 4 sanctity, and anxiously turned in2 patiently
> the pen handed me the answers 2 the questions
> and branded me with protection, almighty blessings

"but watch out, a critic-copper come-a-knockin' and a-testing
arresting every artist confessing 2 a spiritual movement
so, soon we went looking 4 a place where souls weren't 4 rent
time spent on the run like a new born song sung
locked in prison, we just sing-sing
our tribe teaching undercover 2 point out the wrong 1s
long hunt, we bless people with little soul
and those who have none."

> my father told me our jobs will never b done

"u will always b on a re-quest
4 the words that effect
and reset the standards
of 1 word worth a 1000 pictures from a camera
unmatched power in this stanza,
the untapped power in your hands, son
i brandya with soul-melanated black as a panther
and that's worth fighting -- so u will keep writing the word."

"lesson 2: the cup"

"lesson 2: see thru who u r
let there b a release,
piece by peace
ask who breathes in nature's scheme
u or the poe-a-tree
whose roots r more deep
who's supplanted and free
u or the wordz u leave on the paper
scribed from the mind 2 papermate wand,
defended by the saber -- balance your behavior
wordz in the air (there) quickly lose existence
but r bound 2 b sentenced on the page
no parole from this cage,
modern day sage and judge
the papyrus b your cup
empty your mind on2 documents
declare indePENdence
every new thought indented
the cup of a carPENder
the cup of your life
the origin u b from
sacrificed, resurrected, sawed and drummed,
chipped and digested
screened, beaten, rested
stuff treasure chest-ed
your words (by paper) caress-ed
mixed box, wet ended
wire screened, suction boxed
where rolled and felt
the liquid in cup bright like orion's belt
end process: papyrus blessed
cylinder dried, super calendar--rolled pressed
count the days, x-ed off on parchment
your wordz will live long,
many will drink from your cup,
your pen never b tainted --- your wordz will live far pass 4ever
--- when u become ancient."

"lesson 3: the wand"

"after u drink deep and indulge your gift
shift reality until it becomes your wish
with the papermate wand, rewrite it
b the hero in life's script
extend time and make it crypt-tick
tock
a new lock grows 4 every hour u encompass
from this, your frame of mind
can picture the sands of time age like wine
pour what iz in our glass in2 your pen
use this knowledge 2 blend wand and cup
let these 2 bodies make love -- prophesies
see time thru other eyes and dot them

-- document them --

your birthrights of the rite 2 write
and everything u see must b what others read
u the author,
the pen, your key
but there must b more moving on the page than just the pen
u must not let roads end (despite where u were born)
u must extend new 1s 4 infant thoughts 2 come
like wind,
wordz must wind and bend with the wand

-- literary painter --

draw attention with pen and paper
and the wordz they birth thru the womb of the pen's tip
rough against the paper
but does not tear or rip its fabric
hard as moses' laws and tablets
that pen-phone and pen-keg?
tap it
let there b magic 4 u 2 bring 2 the masses
positive adding and negative subtracting
bind by signs and go off on tangents

cosign your life 2 your queen,
let there b no sin

u and her wake up, team up,
let God guide and beam up
so u can create poetry the sandman couldn't dream up
sew all seams up with this wand
(don't wander or squander your thoughts)
the Thought Police will call your magic voodoo
and do vroom! vroom! until they give u room 2 BOOM!
don't let soon b reversed 2 noos(e)
placed around your neck -- silence your culture's breath
but 4 u there iz no death
there iz only life in your pen
your life now,
and your life

        -- next --   lesson will b the sword 2 help u
protect

i scribe becuz all i know will 1 day b new 2 u
'your pen b the voice of a destiny come true'."[1]

---

[1] From the poem, "My Pen" by Rha Goddess

"lesson 4: the sword"[2]

"it iz attached like umbilical
it cuts the wind in a sharp sound
it whispers, vocal
musical, it has its own set of chords
this b the sword

master it thru 5 elements
earth, water, fire, wind, and emptiness
squat and stride legs -- keep balance
battle at close range with sword,
4mation: phalanx

sword hilt 3 inches from your heart -- back straight
eyes facing every direction, inspection of every enemy
so u can see all 3-60 degrees
the observing eye iz stronger,
the perceiving eye iz weaker
look up in peripheral,
God stands above u as your sentinel
aim your sword towards the straight path
level the contour of the earth
and your enemies' advantage will b taken by half

keep your mind and body like water,
fluid with every attack
strike in a flash,
like fire,
swiftly
not really in a high velocity
cuz possible your enemy will counter the attack easily,
your style must b like the wind
strike an opponent down in a single beat
let your body dance and leap
2 the rhythm of the second spring

---

[2] Philosophy composed from "The Book of 5 Rings" by
Miyamoto Musashi

and battle with the fury of all 4 seasons

attack at the sound of an angel's horn,
striking without thought and form
-- the flowing water stroke --
and as it broke u gave birth 2 the chance hit
heavy damage,
the spark hit -- slice thru your target
take your opponent's sword over with the crimson foliage hit
move shadows 2 battle,
knock the heart out and become new
like a rock wall
inaccessible 2 anything at all

-- immovable --

and then there iz emptiness
the realm where nothing exists
where u know and don't know
where u act without acting
without thinking,
where 2 b or not 2 b iz the answer -- sun dancer
where we as warriors and prophets
exist solely in wisdom and logic
all this in a single sword swing
in a plural rhythm of king and queen

un4tunately our will may bring us 2 kill
defend our culture and women
train them 2 fight just the same
4 we as 'us'
r equal in mind, spirit, body, and name
we r nature's lover
we never strike down 1 another
united sisters and brothers, fathers and mothers
we use the sword in defense
as we spread faith 2 bring balance
and set this gruesome world
on the path and direction our swords lay & face:
set this world straight."

"i study 4"

sunlight turned 2 midnight
my thoughts wandering 2 the left
about what i shoud write
enemies i will fight
and allies i will cling tight 2
and who might u b?
which category do u fit under
do u PRAY or hunter -- i wonder?
there iz a battle i need 2 study 4
equipped with word, cup, wand, and sword
but be4 i have at this i'll need 2 practice

>>>roll up sleeve<<<

take pen & paper -- slowly breathe
don't release until tracks r put over me
or until i grow beats in my heart's garden
this world may harden but i'll crack the shell
minds may dry but my wordz will always overFLOW the well
dwell in spaces on pages, create magic thru spells
keep those in need, enlightened
every 7th sense heightened
i am the star that brightens
i am the sun of the titans

--- giants walk this earth ---

i walk in the shoes of those who created gods 1st
and who were 1st created by God -- my clan, my entourage
all-the-way-black mob
our jobs, 2 secure hope 2 those who've been robbed
cut thru our enemies with any weapon in sight
-- swing with God's might --
break our enemies' spirits (with sword) raise yours with lyrics
clear it, the battlefield -- let it rain, bloodstained
the bodies of our enemies' all that remain
little by little, we'll drain the pains of our world
the trinity of the enemy must b broken and fractured

weave a clear thought pattern
          lock our hair
2 b their natural disaster
after we have mastered our 4 lessons
study the wordz of The Father,
          and they will b our greatest weapons

"ceremony"

my clan dance by fire
their spirits burning brighter
than the flame writhing in the middle
i fiddle with sword,
Father Aquarius preach about the state of the world
i watch the girls twirl and swirl in2 the existence of women
they, the wind
i wonder which 1 will turn me in2 a man
hand me virginity
nothing dirty -- yeah, that's right
give me innocence thru a sexual experience
the way it was meant b
                         -- like adam and eve
be4 they ate from the tree

i already have half of knowledge
which 4m will she cum in 2 give me life
i'll slip all five of musashi's rings on her fingers
2 make her my wife
her flesh dressed up in the night sky
see her even when my eyes r closed
she poses thru my prose -- make her cum-posed

love her like nature, even when she's cold
and if she's in summer's heat
i'll b the cold against her body on a hot day
the warm water in her bath
she uses 2 soothe when her bones ache
concentrate and don't b late when it's time 2 come
make time flow and run,
so many 2 hold -- but love all thru 1 --
our spirits burning brighter
her hands dancing around my fire
our embrace tighter,
the night becoming lighter (like my fantasy)

masturbation?
just an emancipation of thoughts i can't express yet

{they will ultimately lead 2 a greater destiny}
so which woman here will it b --- which 1 will give me ... peace ...

"ceremony continued, Thought Police"

it was time 2 define our enemies
Father Aquarius preach about the pain in the axis powers[3]
the battle with them in the last hour
when the world iz showered in souls
tides r shifted, spirits uplifted
the innocent defended by the gifted
our enemies' influence on our world omitted
Father Aquarius gave 2 us their definition:

Thought Police/Thought Cops/Critic-Coppers:
defined as knowledge and history stoppers
ignorant plotters
plotting ignorance
cursing our rebellions, our resistance
their mission 2 erase our existence
burning our books and beating our culture in2 submission
punishing any1 who listens 2 us

the foot soldiers,
the stormtroopers
our history removers
they dim our enlightened

under the guidance and leadership of the Pale King
these troops spring in2 action against our rebel faction
rounding up our culture, history, children, queens, and dreams
they reverse them,
perverse them in2 nigger-slave-bitch themes
they throw them up on movie screens (distorted)
they copy what iz our right
they play our images loud on stereo-types
we've bled 4 their stars and stripes and now they're famous
infamous -- secretly, they worship us

seek our spiritual positions

---

[3] "pain in the axis powers" quote from dennis miller

but they can't b embracers or culture huggers
4 centuries they have been enslavers and settlement
smugglers
not apart of the diversity, the cultural population,
the center of mean
4 centuries they have studied only 1 thing:
reversed al-khem-istry,
put our gold skin behind iron bars,
science fiends
          -- using --
biology to rationalize culture for inferior genes
destroyers and lawyers of a different law -- grave fillers
our blood spillers
stealing wisdom
and driving it right back down the throats of its origin
but our birthrights will always return
and the Thought Police will 1 day repent and yearn 2 unlearn
what they have tried to make us learn

"ceremony continued, The Pale King"

and then came the definition of the pale king
rising from Mother Pisces' voice
rising higher with the fire -- in2 the stars

The Pale King:
he turned gods 2 dogs
wind in2 fog,
clouded our minds
broke nature's spine,
he cut our hair-atage
learned our dictionary
then burned language

burned our libraries
with an offbeat heartbeat, silenced our drums
in2 our kingdom he comes
faked a smile -- learned the songs we sang 2 honor the nile
he sang out of tune
made the sun and moon cry becuz he feared nature
gave our crowns 2 another collective who reaped it -- raped it
all that was sacred invaded
                              -- raided in record numbers
pale king plundered and rebuilt the world
on our knowledge from the age of wonders
we migrated west
but our Mother Land's womb was infested
pale king manifested his own destiny
we pushed 4 moor but our wings were clipped
-- we could not soar --
our blood poured, the tumbling of kingdoms roared

the pale king stole our future child -- piled us up
committed genocide in God's name,

in chains we were taken 2 a familiar land

-- this time stole-land --

the pale king forced us 2 remold it by hand
by our ancient architecture
he took our queens and sack-religiously blessed her
split us up by colour -- light and dark
made us 4get that we were all of 1 melaninated heart
he created a new alphabet
starting with ABC-NBC-CBS -- Pale King re-wrote everything
with Thought Police, every breath of knowledge we released
he seduced us with eMpT.V.[4] sorcery screens
our minds became complacent
made us a science experiment
{had the sum of us in projects}
he was sly as a FOX
disguised with heru's eye
Big Brother-Pale King could CNNeverything
ESPN -- made sports of us -- combatants
Extra Sensory Perception Network
work nets
enter-nets
around our necks on television sets
put our minds at rest
-- worshiped his god 2 believe we were blessed --
and i can no longer BET on jazz
struggling-a-transmission in static and ash

then came self destruction
as he himself began 2 smother
his children killing 1 another -- his brother against his brother
sister against sister
the pale king's stolen land blistered with his own blood

---

[4] bryan thomas (brutha strong)

and as we made love and re-united,
he declared war and tore thru our union
his mentality older than his religion
he envisioned that no 1 but him would control the wind
kill with lightning
inspire fear with great thunder
          -- but nature called 4 our help --
and so,
our giant spirits have awoken from slumber

"ceremony continued, The Shogun"

"the shogun was once 1 of us, son
scared of destiny he decided 2 run
from past lashes he crafted anger in2 a weapon
instead of wisdom
he decided 2 use culture against every1 who looked like him
u see, his mother's nature was 2 leave him
his father's time was spent abusing him
they call him 'nigger'
we figure his origin iz discipline
descended from the repercussions of irresponsible power
placed in a whip that slapped his 4father's back
that broke his language and made him fear an education
2 repair it and keep it intact
he lacks what we have
and wishes 2 per-verse it in his own broken wordz
the shogun was lured by the Pale King's false beauty queen
seduced by the Pale King's nationalistic dream
but the shogun will never b able 2 obtain it
the Pale King has just feigned it,
his interest in the shogun,
[the Pale King has] painted a picture
of perfection 2 learn our lessons and taint our scriptures
reversing it 2 negatives from our beautiful pictures

but the shogun, with his less than half education,
knows only 33 and a 3rd of our secrets
but he and the Pale King have been able 2 piece it
little-by-little, thru spies
that iz why we split our vibes,
scribbles,
and lyrics
in2 all sorts of clusters
keep it far from the hustlers
our actions create confusion
and keep the shogun from learning and using
our knowledge against us
(handing it over 2 the Pale King)

but the shogun only sits lazy,
with nothing on his mind and gold in his mouth
2 make him feel like he's worth something
i don't fear him stealing our magic
cuz he doesn't know how 2 spell
he yells and shouts loud, unable 2 keep his ignorance down
channel it creatively, patiently,
waiting 4 the right moment 4 expression

the tension will begin when this shogun will want 2 call u
'nigger'
until u start acting like 1
and break your language off something proper
properly break it until u r the master's property
instead of mastering it properly. do u follow me?
and with a twirl of his finger,
this ignorant inventor will pull a switch
turn your queen in2 a 'bitch'
and have her at the command of the Pale King's wish
this shogun show's guns as more honorable than the sword
becuz he needs his weapon 2 roar 4 attention
and he does not know how 2 use the pen and the cup
he twists the word, hurls his voice 2 negate thunder
believes he can control the world he stands under
he talks 2 our children and teaches them wrong
sings out-of-tune songs
and the irony b
that with all his foolishness
the Pale King wishes 2 b blessed by him, 2 b like him
it iz the Pale King's children who r the 1st 2 imitate him
and if the shogun continues 2 spread our faith twisted
then our brightest hours will become dim.
and we will b condemned
and we will become damned."

Act II: Training Groundz

"silver on the tree"

2morrow we go
2night we show
what we can mold
as a people
eye see thru peep-holes
windows 2 souls
but don't ask 2 much of me
with all this crafting
i'm still practicing
like my hair,
my wordz still got some kinks
this style ain't as free as u think
we b free 2 think safely
maybe
secretly, pale king praise me
thought police can't evade me
but i can evade them
i frighten them

as much as they want me dead
they still admire the thoughts in my head
and the way i wear my hair, they dread
i spread 4gotten news of millenniums
4 4gotten children
when they chill-drums
shut my mouth!? i'll still speak in morse code hums
even if they murder me i'll liquefy in2 red rum
make stew from my strange fruit
added with the spice of my beats
i'll reign on city streets
shine down and give heat
there iz no meal worth more 2 eat
than the 1 on this silver tree
my roots run that deep

my ancestors are not dead, they just sleep
(as they reside in me)

"steppin'"

creep
creep
creep

we r carried and measured by feet
we beat 4 fun, step in rhythm as we travel
this freedom b louder than shackles
we cackle with the east wind
send thank-you 2 Who B In-charge Up There
just speak in2 the air silent prayers
scitter-scatter like a mouse
use a shadow as a house
when we hear the thought police near
their boots offbeat

BL-U-U-MP
BL-U-U-MP
BL-U-U-MP

we stick close as they hunt
we pray 4 them
if they come across our rhythm and swing
small scuffle, we battle with all 5 rings
2 of 45 survive 2 report back 2 the pale king

creep
creep
creep

we continue sailing
on the air's railing
continue travel with thoughts on our backs
exchange them
frame them in each other's minds
practice our rhymes
4 the time
we r safe in this place between here and there
dressed in all black ancient wear

sum, in a group as 1, snoop -- search 4 new recruits
add them 2 our family tree, teach them their roots
put us on a route that leads us in all directions
we r ubiquitous with our lessons
reciting and writing 42 negatives and confessions
our tribe numbers seven
creep
creep
creep
we steppin'

"in-town chant"

Father Aquarius lets me speak
on the 1st stop
i scream,

"from the top

bald heads or lox
cool air or mops
that scoop up
what stardust drops
corn row crops
our voices rock
set yo clocks
and wrist/watch what i do

we slide right thru and bayou
we've ended up in your neck of the woods
ready 2 break neck speeds
and set it on our new record
brutha strong b a free-may-son
brutha hero dismember in december
editor, inventor, image director
we b art's soldiers
our story's scenes seen in correct order
i was born in the month of a-peril
i always knew there would b struggle

but every transmission made on stereo-types
we scrambled it
made mother nature orgasm
then sampled it
we r father this time
caress nature's spine
heard the earth thru my hair
dangle like grapevines,
this family tree grows sub/lime

sister sunlight, she brave
her smile shines in rays
brutha midnight sparkles with star waves
the moon controls his emotions
the cosmos drips lotion
i catch it and rub it on my queen's back
ancient skin colour, she b my religious artifact
in her eyes and between her thighs
OURstory iz intact

our heavenly bodies 2gether create aura
this iz therapy, we r the past's aroma
descended, african scented
4med from every dimension
mind-body-soul blended
shouting thru time
throwing our lines
2 catch the attention of future generations

fear not,
this iz no invasion
these wordz r free like emancipation
kiss my wordz and understand what i'm tastin'
every time i speak, i eat
the knowledge of the tree -- it's no sin
i can't separate my life from the pen

i'm kickin' it per mission
but without my permission
i believe, u can't sell or buy me

and none of the unholy trinity can defy me
i raise the ruf
and make a fus' 2 say,
don't even dare
my clan got that mathematical equation
I = MCs scared."

"we battle, swordz swinging"

burning trees
and staining grass
pale king made path
he became negative math
reducing nature 2 ash

town invaded
two have be-traded
our lives 4 theirs
they will not live
past this hour

Father Aquarius say,
"let us b the obstacle
in this course.
let us battle with
the light and darkside
of the force.

my people, grab sword
defend this town
from bowing down
2 the pale king as lord."

i pray 2 the moon
let its light b my shield
as i wield sword
on this battlefield
sun come 2 my aid
light covers sword's blade

the 1st i slay with saber
b the 2 traitors
i'll pray 4 them later
sword then cling! clang!
guns boom! and bang!

thought police
swarm on town streets
we meet head on
swing swiftly, head off
lives lost

guns shout
and toss
propaganda
our image
devoured
by slander

town don't believe that
so they strike back
against pale king's attack

town battle with windstaff
thought police suffer whiplash

>>!i am stabbed!<<

the man's name iz Tag

nimble, like dancer
low whispers
call him 'cancer'
becuz he kills slowly
his mind infects body

Tag battles
with spear
sharpened
on both ends
2 frighten

strength and hero
come 2 my side and defend
Tag yells,
"we at odds 'till we even

think u can beat me niggers
u dreamin'.

this 1 has infinite levels
and u may tie
or flip the score
but it'll never b settled."

we reply,
"yeah, but we b the bass
in your treble
the gold u desire
in your bass metal
we the cause
4 every rebel

and u in trouble
next time we rumble
24-7 we at this
concentrate and practice

study our lessons
written on ancient papyrus
yours written on banana peels
cuz u slippin' trippin'
ifin' u thinkin'
u more than our match."

Tag sneers, "niggers,
i'm better than that
i'm faster
than u blinkin'
make 1 false move
and the next time u walk
u'll b limpin'.

don't think the scenario
of me losing this battle
b existin' in the future.
i battle 4 the pale king as ruler."

we 3 eye bruthas retort,
"no man can b ruler
no man can measure up
2 that Great Producer
pale king just a seducer."

dark, lock-haired warrior
jump in2 battle
town resident
he battles with windstaff

his name iz jamaal blackmore
he and Tag battle each other
like they've done this be4
we 3 eye bruthas attack with sword

Tag kicks us back, bored
but he smiles sly, happy
i have 2 admit
his style ain't 2 shabby

but--

beatin' back
off beat
thought police
and Tag
retreat

this town no longer safe
we evacuate and take
the residents
2 a brighter place

so, we still steppin'
off 2 teach others
our ancient lessons

"inner-collective ally, jamaal"

all lies
in this ally
jamaal and i
become quick friends

he knows about
the ancients
we become reminiscent
on a past we've
never been 2

but,
this what the wind do
when u inhale (not what u think)
ancestors cover us
like veils
lead us down
an ancestral trail

we prance thru the trees
balance on every limb
Father Aquarius
will still
teach him
our lessons
keep his life
aimed in
the right direction

our voices
in the wind
we slick talk
about women,
jamaal says his people craft
thru movement
instead of the pen

jamaal's breath enters

thru the west --- Hay Ward guild
taught 2 build
his town filled
with another
ancient knowledge

collected not in
this region
it teaches them
2 b shift shapers
also,
how 2 capture worldly scenes
on paper

i teach him the sword
we spar while speaking jazz
he teaches me
how 2 use
the windstaff

we keep slick talkin'
'bout women
and we laugh
there b peace
we wonder how long
it will last

we make 1 minute vast
time in present
that gift never past
every smooth line
we give props and daps

everything,
4 the moment
b relaxed
cool vibe

we speak spells
that let us pull

wine out of the sky
stardust mixed
with sun rays

our thoughts stray
over the horizon
and we both know
in the distance
where the battle hornz blow
we r allies now,
against
            a common foe

"plan in chant"

our clan destined/plotting and manifestin'
in2 1 solid group,
listening 2 elders addressin'
keep voices low 2 escape detection
we restin' in these woods
swarm around campfire like atoms and eves
weave a pattern like protons and electrons
swirl around neutrons
but we stand still

we gather like space matter
4m 1 collective body

ash scatters/reality shatters
Father Aquarius describes,
his wordz 4m in our eyes
as pictures that guide our thoughts
he tells us about bruthaz and sistas
who've been caught, bought, and brought
2 a place not 2 far from here

"we b in-chanted
jazz move, dancin'
do-rah-me
do rain on me
God give plan 2 thee
our bruthas and sistas
must b set free
reconnected 2 family tree

like Lituolone
we'll do this alone
but in 1 great number
eclipse like penumbra
storm the walls of this 4tress
it's name b kammapa.

attack in sea 4mation

like waves and verse
march in line
after line
unstoppable like the devouring of time
the sun and moon
have said they will not shine

we will b disguised by night
and it will b the star lights
whose eyes we see with
align with mars and venus
love 4 our own
and war 4 our enemy
God has sent 2 me
this battle's outcome in prophecy."

jamaal's voice breaks monotony,
"who possibly will b guarding?
thought police, shogun, or pale king?"

Father voice,
"b prepared 4 all things
make every swing count
count every swing
swift and plenty,
cuz conquest b made
on the ashes of 1s enemies[5] .

we have 5 hours 4 preparation
we head south, stealth walking
from here on out
all talking cease
until we make war 4 peace
let God b with thee."
(and so, we r dismissed 3 by 3 by 3)

---

[5] jason thomas, brutha hero

"we ceremony, handz 2gether"

invoke the ghost
invoke the ghost
invoke the ghost

i am symetry
my hands 2gether
my eyes closed
i see eternity

an amoebae of colours
swirl in2 1 another
on the backdrop of space
the colours turn in2 rain
and they spill on emptiness
i can make out a thousand names
plus more, times seventy-4

jamaal tells me they r the names
of goddesses and queens
they r shaped:

crttw
btty
arthw
rsw
trw
pyhnw
lrw
rntw
lrn
tmrw
nkw
mxn
kndrw
s'zn
mjry
yshw
tnshw

nnjlw
nyw

and thousands more
all connected 2 eve
i tell the names,

'i am a prayer
i am a prayer
there in the lips
spoken in the air
i am a prayer
unspoken but shared
the concealed 1
a man
amen
amon
i am the sun -- the Son of Suns
atum
the atom
split from eve
and i believe
that 1 day u and i will conceive
the tree of knowledge from our roots
and gain 4ever life
keeping our hearts right
and holding on 2 all we have left
every other breath -- a prayer'

i act on a whim-amun
sun in feminine 4m
weapon and armor
4hundred years without breath
could not harm her

she gives me power
i have less than an hour
2 prepare
goddesses say,

'i b that 1st word spoken in the beginning,
i am the 1st prayer
and i am bare, leaving u naked
and my truth b hard 2 digest
but u must regress -- regress so far back
and become the original name God blessed u with
-- african --
that iz a real revolution
i am not Jesus, i am just resurrection
the lesson, spoken by the blessed son
cuz i b the 1
i am a prayer'

"we ceremony, handz apart"

palm open,
up,
face heaven
heaven face
up
open palm
receive the twilight's song
when dusk iz equal 2 dawn
sun makes final peek,
be4 it sleeps beneath
the horizon
now we have an open-eye orison
as our thoughts begin risin'
                              --- mind glidin'
jamaal enlightens,
'open mind wide
don't b shy
God does not exist in the sky
and sometimes
u can see God with the physical eye
God walks on air at times
but not 2 high
i'll past the word 2 u, kheru
so u can get on the vibe'

in the middle of circle
middle of tribe
i recite without scribe,

'i prosper and live long
my fire set off every alarm
but i cool down the fire
2 make a woman come real strong'

crowd shout loud
i continue
under their cloud,

'Tag may stab
but he ain't got the rhythm
2 beat me
i shake everyday
like some1 tryin' 2 beep me
curse his existence
my testimony b sworn
i b diamond month born
i'm a woman's best friend
playin' the field
like miles played his horn
if the sky b my mother
then earth b my father
i b the son who shine on u 'till the day b done
we don't lose,
the number on this act b won
when it comes 2 the thought troops
we loop-loop and keep the beat on the run'

"we ceremony, clap in chant"

we rhyme assistin'
in this soul kitchen
party as we drink stardust
be4 we act out our mission
this iz how we work it
descendants of the chitlin' circuits
sippin' on pop daddies
and glam slams
we break dance
repair by prayer and chants

clap
clap
we take u across the map
clap
clap
we take u across the map

in psalms we break free from trap
pale king say our culture has us wrapped
we free from that
our minds settled back
we in the past now

clap
clap
we r across the map
clap
clap
we r across the map

the situation unwrapped
change the present
it is 2 tense
we r the honored
the heaven sent
descendants
of the blameless

burnt faced ancients
future and destiny re-shay-PENed
something old has been awakened in us
in justice we will fight injustice
live by the code number 68:31
we have spread our arms out wide from
   -- where we were
   -- 2 bring u the word
our wisdom iz precision
3rd eye in focus, acute vision

clap
clap
we on the map
clap
clap
we on the map

let's back track
rewind the track back
the number on this 1
iz blackjack
define relativism
pessimism iz the wordz of a realist?
i ain't feelin' this
split it thru the prism
make it a rainbow of optimism
but that b the wordz of a child
the nile iz how i flow

4 certain proof
truth b wordz from bartenders
so how 'bout a drink?
2 rethink the year thru december
cleanse me from bein' drunk
of ignorance's remix
life's game ain't fixed
but 4 a while i felt
the cards i was dealt were marked
not like verola --

as it turns out, i'm the card holder
and war's got my back 2 keep peace intact
and what iz past iz last night's memory
more 4 me as i morph with thee
i thought about my own destiny
pale king tried 2 tell me it was fantasy
i reshaped it 2 turn it in2 reality
now the past b in back of me
my eyes focus, i see straight thru ya
and i feel the presence of the present
unwrap it, and behold the future

so clap on that, black
make sure it's on the beat
melanate/meditate
and relax

"battle of kammapa"

we r in plane sight
hidden by the night
the night our ally
we, the stars in the sky
split in2 constellations
we prepare 4 invasion
we drop like rain
attack cold like snow
the wind guides us 2 the earth
we land, gently
the earth cracks, splits
opens up 2 devour our enemies
this iz all done silently
we rise back in2 the night sky
divide in2 stars
we r patient

we move 2 the south entrance of the 4tress
gate open
we descend from the heavens
twenty-seven plus eighteen guards
we as stars, set
like the 4th seal,
we come like death
put 2 rest
every thought troops' breath
we enter kammapa
the belly of the beast
we r digested

from kammapa's lungs,
the deep,
steal beast breathes
another fleet emerges as we creep
we split in2 groups of 3

(well ... truthfully ... we got 4
myself, strong, hero, and jamaal blackmore)

we duck in2 adjacent halls and doors

we dodge the enemy
until we come across 1
we attack quickly,
remove him of his gun
and be4 he can shout
we grapple him,
cover his mouth
place sword's blade against his neck
i ask,
"where r our kindred kept?"
his eyes, wide, terrified,
he answers in a single breath
"in the 3rd sublevel of our 4tress."

our people below consciousness
i knock the thought cop out of it
ghost thru
we go thru
descend
we hear screaming
violent
no light shines in this wasteland
people walk aimless
in circles
we rain purple
in hopes of giving them more colours

[we pray]

the room iz filled
with the presence of thousands of women
their spirit 4m 1 goddess
come 2 teach wisdom and logic
free our people from bondage
pull them up above consciousness
they need 2 breathe
mother pisces lead
thru her, every woman speaks

mother pisces preach
teach
how 2 keep their knowledge sharPENed
how 2 become in-light-and enDARKened
thru soul, body, and mind
see all colours with every opened eye
b on -- and -- in time
history in the making
master the art of destiny shaping

and now,
from kammapa
we all plan on escaping

retracing our steps
we meet up with the rest
father aquarius give praise
our kindred have been saved

-- but --

the thought police attack
en masse
in 1 last
full
force
wave

their screams
a bloodthirsty craze

i sway from their line and fire
we r outgunned, and outnumbered
we remember we can control the thunder
we use it 2 throw our enemies back
lightning bolt lash
we slash
thought police number cut by half

jamaal and i r cut off from clan
forced back in2 another section
we continue dance steppin'
round our enemies
they r confused
as we move with the wind
in rhythm
sword and windstaff visions
dancing in our enemies' eyes

2 keep instep
we recite on beat
2 beat thought police
but they come in swarms
as 1 iz cut down
it looks like another iz born
but we react quickly,
adapt and attack viciously
my sword iz now the colour of rust

the thought police attack in rush
we slide in2 adjacent room,
cut chord,
door slams
cutting the troops off from us

whew! we take a breath

we search 4 another way out
the door creeps up slowly

slowly

      slowly

         slowly

quickly --- we find another door
and we r thru
thought police enter room

they shoot,
guns boom
a quick recite of wordz
and we speed-increase
we become a blur
and merge with the outside

kammapa iz in flames
i concentrate,
receive the names
of those slain
it iz only few
the rest have escaped

the thought police come from the fire
their bodies burning
nature distorted, turning
they scream with mouth and gun
we run in2 4est
our clan iz safe on the other side
our powers weak and dampened

-- we cannot reach them --

a dark voice whispers,
'u r beaten.'
jamaal and i look up
we r surrounded,
no where 2 run
i expected Tag 2 own the voice
but it was the shogun

he orders,
'drp yo' wep-unz 'n' cum.'
we r bound and gagged
dragged behind shogun's tattered rags

he iz dressed in fads and cliches
bright 4 attention
not 2 honor the sun's rays

his skin iz a scab
scratched, scarred, and ash

captive! we follow him … on a long journey back 2 his kingdom "bang on drums"

in cage
housed
with
inmates

jamaal
and i
refuse
2 b slaves 2 this condition

a 3rd of us r here

the repercussions
of our capture
iz just percussion

we begin 2 bang

bang, bang, bang//bang on drums//not with guns//we write and
type//on the surface of the sun//we absorb it's paper thru
melanin

jamaal and i trapped
in shogun's kingdom

this place iz bass distorted//power and thought
dampened//but our hopes run rampant//we let other inmates
sample it//shogun can't tamper with it//how can i make my
voice louder? i still hold an ounce of power//shogun has chosen
us 2 die//we have only 5 hours 2 live//so, we reminisce

but the past iz 2 far
beyond these bars
and my eyes sting
my voice can't sing
i cough and choke
on the smoke that iz this kingdom

not kingdom -- prison

it has my vision distorted//shogun serve's a religion
imported//by the man who imported him//stole his wisdom//i
scream, 'keep your distance.'//my mission takes precedence//i
am the evidence of your crime//i am the voice of time that can
no longer speak//but it seeks judgment//wasn't it u who viewed
my mind thru a kaleidoscope's eye and had the nerve 2 call it
repugnant?

even i can see, that down deep,
the pale king's soul can b sunny
and my vision isn't exactly twenty-twenty

shogun bounces in
the word 'nigger'
dripping off of him
as he dances with a limp
he pimps ignorance

"bitch
don' spread dat wise shit
cuz i'll cut off both dem lips.
dis ain't no muthafuckin'
church choir"

i whisper,
"the word 'education' 2 u
iz like a cross 2 a vampire."

"u have 5 hours
2 take dat back."

"2 late
it's in the past
and i can't time travel."

shogun says,
"dat's awite
y'r judgment

cums at dhe end
o' my gavel.
'less u can give me
dhe whereabouts of your clan."

"if i am 2 put them in your hands
let me tell u in chant
i'll tell u
in the next room
give u wisdom, knowledge, and truth."

needless 2 say
the shogun was seduced

"y' bes' cum wit'
dat shit
--- dhe wurd,
sword, pen, and wand."

he opens cage,
his men shackle me
i walk passivly
but alert
ready 2 take action

shogun leads me in2 beat room
but it's offbeat
talk iz weak
no 1 here can speak

the shogun sits,
not patiently
but still --- waiting 4 me 2 speak

"yo clan?
yo knowledge?
yo life?"

"all in chant."

"all hours in a day, all iz ours"

shogun yells,
"y' lessons
y' knowledge
y' clan."

>>pause<<

i speak,
"i am more than human
and less sun
i am your lesSun
number 1
i shine brighter
than guns r loud
while sleeping on clouds."

"nigga,
will u make sense?"

"and b a sellout!?
i will not make cents 4 change
i am 4 by 90 degrees
intersecting 7 planes
what's your range? shooting?
simply A 2 B?
i am magnetic of all active energy

and out of all the swords
my tongue iz the sharpest
i was produced from triple darkness
mother, father, God
the pale king's target
i am 2 hours younger than these wordz

i am the 2nd tenth hour."

"butchu only got 5 hours 2 live.
take dis bitch away. give 'im 2 magikkk."

Act III: Take a Right 2 Passage

"magikkk"

enchantress
all implanted
fake
no soul
tampered with

she writhes like snake pits
whore of babylon
who dances on -- music blasted on stereo-- (y'know)

she dances 2 the beats
of nigger songs
trampling on isis's image
she seduces children
who sample on her breast
it drips acid
burns their vocal chords

magikkk devoured her father's son
as he set in the west
she caressed the 666 beast
as he fed upon the weak

she tied jesus down
that's why i weep
jesus lay raped
his orginal name 4saked
his original face painted over
the falcon morphed 2 a dove
wings clipped -- unable 2 soar
and his mother, 'madonna'
iz synonymous
with the word 'whore'

crucified on magikkk's body
religion iz her property
i'll stay ancestrally faithful
as i'm tied in this chair

she dances around bare of soul

she tells me she can inject God in my veins
suck shame out of my life
just ... put out the light and then ...
cut like othello's knife
choke like his grip
and take a sip of her breast
acid infested

she slithers
says i'm hers
4 30 pieces of silver
and all my secrets

a snake creeps and hisses
from between her legs
and she begs,
"rape me, nigger, rape me.
i'll tell no 1, just rape me."

instead i pray 4 her
shogun says i'll die earlier

"bring dat nigga, jamaal."

jamaal doesn't give in either
shogun begins 2 beat her,
magikkk,
she enjoys it
shogun ignores her -- that annoys her

"black on black, african vs. nigger"

surrounded
bound
but not gagged
5 thought police
shogun in center
guns aimed

jamaal and i stand firm

"God iz now in our veins
and we will remain
even though death may change
the physical appearance."

shogun yells,
"quiet!"

i voice,
"i will not b quiet
my mouth will shout riots
this may seem like a freestyle
but God iz my sponsor
behind my eyelids scroll a word monitior
but pale king monitor the wordz behind my eyes
edit and revise them until they r lies
now they're the tears i cry
but even when closed, i see thru another eye

shogun, my brutha, r u blind?
don't u see they've taken your lines
connected with your past time
and u still playin' games on their field?

pale king praise u
only 2 play u
but it's all right
as long as he pays u

u bow 2 his green paper
worship it
as if it had the picture
        -- of your savior scrawled on it

i cry-o-my-genetics
tears frozen in time
ancestors caress my spine
swinging on thoughts like vines

pale king has scratched your rhymes
made them hard, gritty, c-c-c-crimes
left your body outlined in chalk
and u ask, 'where iz everybody?'
everybody's bodies sleeping
leaning against poles
drunken, stumblin'
wake up! smell what they shovelin'
it's your ashes
history burners, icon-o-classicist

smoke ancient wordz
not the earth's herbs
it's absurd,
your high iz the sun in the sky
will u take that knowledge 4 a bride?
or your people's lives as a bribe?
understand it was the pale king
who turned your kingdom in2 a savage tribe
that's his math
but we r greater as half
than his troops in full mass
we outcasts ride

vibe on ancient pride
and if that b suicide in pale king's eyes
then let me constantly die
as u help him commit genocide

but i die and revive

so smooth that thoughts don't fly
they glide
ride the air delivering dreams
dreamwaves in airwaves
channel soul and let u tune in
absorb melanin so u can b black again
thru al-khem-istry

turn an old being in2 a nu-being (nubian)
turn clear air, soul gold carbon and oxygen
burnished brass like Jesus' skin
put the **hue** back in every **man**
shape every queen out of africa's darkest sands
and bathe u in the sun beams
so u can understand how the sun dreams

that masculine/feminine inspiration
of the GOD 'HE/SHE/ORIT'
who put my thoughts in orbit
and created the stars

that's why u think i'm so bright
i shine against the night
and if u look up
at the constellations just right
u'll understand stand
they're just my name
up in lights

and they get brighter
as i meditate on jazz
reciting the blues
my voice carving rock
in the temple of funk
i b a shaolin/thelonius monk."

the shogun trembles
jamaal chants,

"my heart and soul iz not 4 ransom

my hair make me handsome
pale king ask,
'what's that on your head son?'
so i tell 'em,
'something 2 get me closer 2 the sun
i call it culture
hey shogun, i notice u ain't got none.

let me break the chant down so low
u'll b able 2 hear the grass grow
my hair b a 4rest
on every vinelock
there's a fruit called 'chorus'
so let's sing

shogun,
unlike most bruthas
u cut your hair out of self hatred
not 2 feel nature's kiss, sacred
her wind can't b tasted
rubbin' against baldness
or tickling the dreads
yeah,
your mother nature
gives good head

if u see fit,
let me rest 6 ft. deep
in the earth's bed."

BANG!

BANG!

BANG!

BANG!

BANG!

but when we open our eyes
the 5 thought troops lie dead
we r unbound
our weapons on the ground
it iz quiet
sigh lent peace

"go,"
the shogun's voice echoes
power in a single syllable
"go, my bruthas, go.
chant, and go."

wind becomes sound
becomes traces of matter
becomes the shogun's shadow
he understands nature
his power true
his flesh renewed
a man of hue

"go," he repeats.

"come with us."

"it's ... 2 late 4 me.
take the inmates with u."

changed, he reveals his true name,
"my name iz seth. now GO!"

"more than that,
u r us.
we r u.
family,
heritage,,
culture,
allies against a common foe."

we disappear
our powers revived
we take the inmates
and escape in2 the night

"dancing in freedom"

dancing in freedom
iz skipping with the rain
that's what we do
cuz freedom reigns on us
we jam on ziggy
stardust drinkin'
these inmates have never known this freedom
and we owe it 2 seth?
as he wept
he let the sons of the earth free
and set
murderer of his brother osiris
he became more from less
redeemed thru a promised kept
he let the sons of the earth free
chant with me,

"osiris, your brother iz free
the pale king no longer holds him
and so your descendants' sons rise
their daughters, absorbed like the water
and when it rains they fall on us
when the sun shines, we r warm from them
we r the descendants of the sun and rain
and let freedom shine and reign
we pray 4 an enemy who iz now our ally"

i tell jamaal,
"once we find our clan
we'll go back and rescue the rest
including seth."

"do u suspect a trap?"

i retort,
"no man
could ever
wield nature

like that
if he weren't truly free
in mind, and spirit."

we continue
dancing
chanting
nature, raining
clouds sparsely populate the sky
the sun jacks up
backs up in2 the sky
bouncing 2 our vibe
its rays embracing the clouds
its voice scatting like jazz

i wonder who woke up who

"3 beat search, 2nd end 4"

jamaal's eyes
understands
what they see
he stands under
over trees

he takes sword
(that is pen)
and invokes
the world on
paper. he draws

his legs touch
earth. we search
the world drawn

jamaal knows
where 2 go
the inmates,
they follow

our clan iz
near. we can
hear them. we
rush 2 them.

we r free
our journey
at an end

"ra union"

in the center
where trees
4m 3-60 degrees
where the sun's rays
and the earth meet
there was a faint beat

a beat of heart and drums
people chanting as 1
there, in the clearing
a distance away
but a ray of light extended
and like a bridge we crossed
we ran
reunited with clan
rushed in2 open arms and hands

brutha br-eye-on, strong
brutha jah-sun, hero
mother pisces, and her legion
queens, goddesses, women
father aquarius
and the warrior class mass

we narrate our flight
jamaal acts it out
as i recite
our run from the shogun
i surprise father aquarius
--as well as everyone--
when i orate the shogun's redemption
i call him by his true name, seth
and say that the rest of his kingdom
must b rescued

"jamaal can lead us back
he has scribed map
and with our forces intact

we could push back pale king's attack
if this iz in fact just a trap."

father aquarius shakes his head
"the shogun's spirit iz dead.
seth's voice and soul iz true
we must plan rescue
and embrace him as a new recruit."

we rest a day
cultivate the inmates
educate them thru the 4 lessons

we rest a day,
settle back,
hold ceremony
and pray
the men invoke the spirit
of the women -- 4 strength
the women invoke the spirit
of the men -- we blend
2morrow we'll fight with double strength
we'll battle 2 the end
2night we sing a warrior's song
2morrow, we attack at dawn

"kingdom come"

we march
across horizon
as the sun comes up
we march

every mountain becomes a plain
every plain a valley
and we descend
every ray of light blends with us
only us, just us
we r here in the name of justice
we march

in2 fog and clouds
smoke and flames
we will rain on this kingdom
and we can feel the presence
of the reigning king
we can hear screaming
inmates bleeding
pale king keeping them down
tortured, bound
we shatter all barriers with a single sound

faced-2-face with time
we r 2 late
we see seth has met fate
swords and spears pierce his body
4mation: cross
truly 1 with the spirit he had lost
nailed 2 a wall
his blood trickles down, crawls
          creeping in the adjacent corridor,
seth's murderer calls,

"and now
death has come
2 u all!"

the thought police
fill
the halls

"u'll all die
that iz the way
and there iz no way
2 change it."

my sword turns red
from silver
in a situation all 2 familiar
tag stands at a distance and laughs
father aquarius carves a path
thru the thought police
and attacks him
brother strong and hero take action
as the rest of us r trapped in
battling the thought police
we do not accept death or defeat
fight with a beat and beat them back
new inmates join the attack
1 named rufus
who speaks and builds
a magical shield around his body
next 2 him iz a giant --- sha-nun,

dreads so long, they wrap around his neck
inset with jewels and gold bands,
sha-nun fights hand-2-hand
bare hands -- strength of a bear
the heir of a fighting style
           that helps us tear thru the opposition

my vision catches tag and father aquarius,
strong, and hero battling vicious
tag holding them at bay
every sword swing and sway
dodged and parried

tag separates the melee
strong and hero r kicked away from the fray
tag and father aquarius clash

-- i dash in their direction --

brutha hero knocked in2 a different section
strong and i keep pressin' on

mother pisces shines like the dawn
she takes father aquarius' side
battling tag 2gether
raining on him like weather
but they become severed
tag iz 2 malicious
he lashes out, vigorous
he becomes graceful,
like a dancer
this man, tag,
nicknamed 'cancer',
captures time and attacks

father aquarius
iz fatally
stabbed

mother pisces iz consumed with tears
she iz paralyzed with fear

tag ... disappears,

his laughter echoing
settling in our minds

late, we arrive
3 bruthaz,
derived from the 3 i's
of our father aquarius -- who has died
the stars have negatively aligned
cancer in aquarius

every scar deepened
i am consumed by 1 word
i have been reduced 2 1 sense,

revenge

while this maniacs laughter

echoes,
          echoes,
                    echoes,
                              echoes,
                                        echoes,
                                                  echoes,
and settles

          (settles)
                    (settles)
                              (settles)

in my mind

"ra group"

with the inmates we escape
take a different route and regroup

more have joined us
much more taken away
and we can't stay here
jamaal fears his inner vision
it can see the pale king
          -- marching in the distance
an army of thousands
marching with him
off beat chanting
off beat dancing
the day has turned
2 dusk from dawn

i see mother pisces,
she lies still
in brutha hero's arms
father aquarius
cradled in strong's grip
his life and breath exist
          -- only in the past
that iz no more than half my age
in minutes ...

father aquarius iz still back there
somewhere, still,
his last air fills a room
an escaped breath rests
possibly without understanding
that its life iz now death
but knowing that great man
he understands
and stands over us
we r his last heirs
we r his remaining breath of life

but do we run
or fight?

revenge is all that remains in my veins
i want 2 take this pain
and rain down on the pale king
send him back whence he came

my heart a furnace
heat and hatred
pump thru me
land on my tongue
and i can taste it

i lick my lips
sip revenge
as it drips,
drips
drips

it bleeds thru my wrists
as i grip my sword
i want 2 pour this feeling
on2 the pale king

i look up
my clan looks at me
waiting 2 set them free
pale king iz closer
          -- in jamaal's vision
and it iz me
who must make a decision

"we must flee 2 safety
find sanctuary
and regroup our thoughts."

we take flight
blend in2 the night
this act,
closed curtain
our future
uncertain ...

"the burial"

the sun's rays dimmed
except 1, extended from the center
extended down 2 him
father aquarius
as he lay buried
the moon's light dripped,
trickled in2 the clouds
it rained all day

even nature wept
4 our father's
eternal rest

we harmonized
in a single breath
addressed the greatness
that was father aquarius
and the various areas he touched

he iz now a spirit we invoke
cover his grave with a rose
his spirit flows in2 space
touches the moon, sun, and stars
knows no distance that iz far
beyond land and sea
he iz me
we r a triple trinity
2997, 999
he iz space and time
soul and mind
no longer rewind
we r 4ward
press play
father aquarius now prays
with a long list of descendants

does that sound pretentious?
well it's not pretense

be4 tense
future, past, present
i am pro tense
professional tension
released thru revenge
in the spirit of my father i will defend
end the life of the pale king
          -- and his henchman named tag
becuz moon-water light rains prematurely
early, on our father
who art in heaven,
buried in the earth
verse-by-verse
with the power of the moon
the climate will reverse
and like the waves,
father aquarius' spirit will ascend

my knees will never bend
un-less in prayer
prayer in less-un
remember,
the ancient voice iz where i am from
until the day when all r 1 and won

"4ward"

we pace
in the same place
behind time
in this race
mother pisces face iz still
her eyes still closed
her body frozen
mind shattered and broken
paralyzed with sorrow's emotion

our own minds not open
focused on loss
caught in past tragedy
we have actually become still
filled with ill wills
our will is gone
we must sing resolution's song

but brutha strong and hero
r at each others' throats
we choke on our own tension
friction
it causes smoke
we cannot breath
and i must leave
so that i may b at rest
a new quest
paved with blood
and the death of the pale king
drown him with the power of the sea-king
i am seeking revenge

my clans' actions descend
i must continue 4ward
past the border of the past
understand it
ally with it
and use it 2 battle

i rattle like a snake
venom in my mouth
i shout a thousand curses
and worship my own anger

my father's lessons
and actions become fainter
i divide them by my emotions
and only come up with 1 remainder

so, as i sit here and weep
i must make a simple choice
do i battle with sword,
or the wand,
with cup,
word,
and voice?

"sword vs. pen"

i drop pen at my right foot
and sword at my left
and wonder which way i should step

which weapon do i leave at the door?
iz the pen mightier than the sword?
life iz even
but it's not fair
if the pale king and tag take what's mine
i'll take what's theirs
cuz i'm the man who tamed the night mare
turned it in2 a day dream come true
true of voice, i am maa kheru

in dreams
in mind
in reality

i have the pale king after me
like i was butch cassidy
but i don't sun-dance, kid
i dance with the sun
become selfish in some situations
and eclipse it
natures scales, i tip it
poetry verses i flip it
alphabet soup, i sip it
regurgitate my art 2 your plate
my wordz satiate
your knowledge i can inflate
but how do i comPENsate
when matters complicate
1 weapon left at the door
i no longer hold pen in unskilled hand
i hold sword

my thoughts r so low
they're chained 2 the flo'

and flow
and flow
my actions
inspired by past action and hate
but wait!
fog makes my thoughts dissipate
my head iz just in the clouds
ubiquitous in all time zones
except the here and now
and that iz how i block the light from the sun

but the pen keeps running 2 my hands
it demands that i brand every paper
taper, dance, prance
let wordz become vapor
positive thought shaper
and remove negativity from present and future
the pen tells me 2 b calm
b like kama sutra
pen in different positions when scriptin'
shiftin' gears
remove the tears and fears of those near u
make sure they can hear u
or at least read u
so they can b u
and u them
defend -- seek revenge only with pen

bring soul 2 hell's kitchen
pick fights with disorder
damnation, and affliction
and the rest of the pale king's children
these thoughts have me far past the border
and miles from redemption
under the veil of my clan
come the pale king and his henchmen
sweat and laughter breaks the tension
in my finger there's contraction
like an orgasm
but ...

i left my weaPEN at the door
iz it the sword that iz mightier?
pen missing from its holster
but i hold sword as a reinforcer

pale king took what gave me life
but God has father aquarius' soul
so, there iz no wear
life iz even
and the sword
can make it fair
but should i leave pen at the door?
have
just sword?
no pen and pamphlet
like hamlet, i stall
thoughts fall
the future iz inertia

i must act
i take a breath

pen at my right foot
sword at my left
so, where do i step?

sword vs. pen

"my world can either b healed
or damned
at my whim
at --- my --- whim"[6]

---

[6] Blood Omen: Legacy of Kain

"inner-collective allies, pt2"

my eyes pan
            -- my clan
stands still
walking in circles
they argue about revolution

but two stand out
silent yet loud
against the commotion

#1,
sha-nun
shines with sun
dark complexion

so dark he gives
a cool, blue vibe
that dances
with the tide

his hair grows in strides
tied around his neck
decked and inset with jewels,
he manifests the finesse of a warrior
his hair striking chordz with gold bands
his weapon iz the cup
the fist, the hand

he comes from the west
lost angels, less of breath
but he iz more, soars up
2 direct the stars
this dark knight has traveled far
blessed with the copper eRAH
nickname 'kodojo'
we flow
flow
in conversation

i do my best 2 teach him
the 4 lessons
he listens
as i stumble on my wordz

i say,
"like masons
we build on
the ancients
adjacent 2
what iz in us
a pyramid
that starts with the 1st
and spreads back 2 us
then descends back up
when all r 1."

next 2 sha-nun iz rufus
he iz wordz in physical 4m
adorned with precise pronunciation
an inundation
overflow of wordz that drip from pages
and spill over
            until u find
                        them crawling
                                    on2 your page
creeping out
his voice originates from the south
his job iz 2 travel the pen & paper route
as he reverberates like a cloud
his voice rains,
builds a shield around his body

>>pause<<

place a break in space
2 split the monotony
his silence iz even heard,
the weapon iz the word
his thoughts b happy and nappy

these r exactly the people 2 help me
i take them aside
and we devise
a plan
in chant
jamaal
rufus
sha-nun
and i
become a new clan

4 warriors,
we
take
stance

"the divide"

like an atom
we split
like a pair of lips
          -- ready 2 speak
i become anxious
          -- b4 we proceed
i believe i can't leave
my clan in disarray
as i stray away
questions surround me
like the thought police

i pray 2 seek an answer
in the manner of speaking,
kneeling,
knees against the soil
i ask,

"father,
how can i remain loyal
and break away all 2gether?"

and the clouds rain letters
they 4m wordz
tell me 2 pick who will lead the clan in my absence
i pick the warrior named D'win
i know i can trust him
i tell him,

"keep an eye on mother pisces,
and see that strong and hero stay calm."

he nods,
wishes us luck, and we disappear
2 bring 4th a new dawn

"from worshiping lips"

fire had lost breath
and melted, exhausted
smoke lingered in great mass
seth's palace reduced 2 ash

i stand on the spot
where father aquarius
            -- was slain
and i remain still
until i speak a prayer

but on this spot
the past iz here
i step away
we continue
past seth's palace
beyond familiar boundaries

a place where stories and legends
tell of the pale king's influence
his confusion and plagues rage
he fills space with his presence

his own lessons
fill space
but empty
just
the
same

but in small circles
in whispers
people speak of saviors
not of us,
but the pale king's traitors
camp raiders
burning star dust
until the air tastes the flavor

and behind the whispers
spoken by careful speakers
cautious listeners
there are worshipers of our craft
worshipers of an outer collective mass
our black has attracted more than the sun

as we pace we come across
           -- an outer collective
we r cautious
but they give us sanctuary
(despite our difference in colour)
we wonder if this iz but a ruse
but they give us news
insight 2 pale king's loop
1-track on his mind
he has tried 2 record our lines
our wisdom
our lessons, legacy
stolen in his heist
sold at a higher price
he has less than half

but he keeps us in his sights
he has his sights set on our clan
our minds' land in demand
and now that we have new command
pale king thinks he can negotiate
associate amongst us
he knows father aquarius
           -- lies six feet under us
and as we r out here,
seeking revenge as justice,
his silk tongue tickles D'win's ear
his wordz as cool as winter
i fear D'win may become frostbitten
           -- freezer-burned and turned

but have we traveled 2 far out?

can we go back?
i wonder if we would b outnumbered
our clans' minds parallel 2 the pale king
assimilating in hopes of a truce
unaware of the noose slowly placed around their necks

jamaal, rufus, and sha-nun volunteer 2 check
i contemplate our next move
i know pride iz all i have 2 lose
revenge iz still in my left hand
(some would say i ain't in my right mind)
but i know the next time i see tag,
he
dies

i tell the others 2 go back
keep their distance and listen
pay close attention 2 the situation

i will continue with my mission
when it comes 2 tag
i'll handle him … alone

"duel of providence"

i can see him --
standing against the wind

it swirls around his body
never touching
he stands apart from nature
but gazes up,
2wards heaven,
as if he's actually going there

his prayer iz a jumble of wordz
slurred -- unintelligible curse
and what's worse,
his verse iz the song
that brought me here

this clearing,
this field
where smog and fog
eclipse proper thought

but thru the haze
i can see tag clearly
long hair,
glistening
like gold strings
on a magical harp

his white visage blemished
       -- with scars
covered with war paint
a mockery of indian saints
the original warriors of this stole-land
and set in tag's head
black eyes -- burning with hate
they scrape my image
overcast, his pupils, gray clouds
shady,

dismal,
like unpolished gems

i raise my sword 2 him
he raises his weapon
a double-edged lance
tag speaks b4 we dance:

"i confess,
gladly,
dressed in a smile.

i raped the queens
of 1000 cultures
swarmed around like a vulture
captured them 4 labor
had them raise my children
who would rape them later
i savored on the breast, thighs, and leg
held them down 2 hear them beg,
fed on their flesh
until culture rested in my veins

i claimed kingship thru fiendish acts
ripped children from their culture's womb
so that i may get back
2 what should have given birth 2 me

oh! did i reveal my own reality?
my dark tinge of jealousy?
jealous of the dark, indeed

i hate black
becuz i am not black
and i'll kill 2 b that
as well as make lies facts
2 have the whole world
hate u as much as i do
and i have tricked u
your people,

mothers,
fathers,
sisters,
brothers,
lovers
tricked them 2 kill 1 another

i fixed every court trial
and put the whole world in denial
while my hands,
around your neck,
choked u of your last breath
took your culture's wealth
and gave it 2 some1 else
if i could not rightfully own it myself
and i have never felt guilt

hold your sword firmly at the hilt
cuz i will cut u in half
without your nigger beat
or your nigger rhythm
u, my next victim,
i will slay u like i did your father,
a fool with a dream
his life wasted, spent
and
u
          --MOCK kheru--
r
no
different."

i become hell bent on revenge
i attack in a flash
fierce,
deadly,
quickly,
tag parries,
moves my sword aside,
takes a stride 4ward

and swings,
brings 1 end of his lance up
-- i duck --
his attack glides over me
i stand firmly,
block an attack aimed at my back
and quickly shield my front
2 block the brunt of another blow
i push his weapon away -- sway
and throw flurries like snow
but he adapts and flows smoothly
moves me back,
retracts his weapon
and attacks with his feet
he forces me 2 retreat -- withdraw
fall back
my mind iz not intact
in its rightful place
i stall,
silent ...

focusing 2 much on revenge
i cannot remember my lessons
even with the sword in my hand
i have no real weapons 2 fight with

i am the ebb in this flow

tag grows impatient
he initiates conflagration
i take a step,
skip,
twirl,
and advance
my sword clashes with his lance
sparks explode
like warm air slamming against cold
thunder rolls
our bodies glow
mine bright like gold

his dull and 6000 years old
wrapped in oppression
and 7 deadly confessions

the power of our battle
makes the earth split,
and spit flames
the soil becomes scorched,
the wind howls, as earth iz in pain

the land rises
our fight heightens
we duel like fates,
tag makes a fatal move
i block the attack
... but ...
my sword shatters on impact,
          ... it breaks ...

i drop the hilt and await ... my fate ...

tag kicks me back,
the land risen,
i drop off the edge
my hands grip the ledge

and
              i

                      hang

tag towers over me
fire boiling below me
my grip slipping slowly

--- QUICKLY ---

tag turns,
battles another
the earth rumbles
a disastrous war zone

i understand
i am no longer alone

tag's clash
iz with a better half
shadow cast figure
there iz a shimmer of light
hope insight,
but my eyes fight 2 stay open
my strength struggles 2 focus
i hold on2 the edge
with all strength left

and i can hear tag scream,
"my hand! my hand!
u bitch! u cut my hand!"
he screams and retreats

a gentle hand catches me
feminine,
yet rough
--i mean, and i'm talkin'--
tough enough 2 battle tag

she lifts me up

my savior
once my creator
her spirit
populated 57,280,000 miles
her description,
like christ from the bible

sun blessed,
she iz rah dressed, not a shadow
it iz her flesh
i hold on2 her
lose breath
and ultimately
consciousness

saved by this mysterious,
african goddess,
this warrior,
still seeking revenge
4 now,
i can rest

Act IV: Tide Turner

"sentient"

i awake with the sun in my face
rather, a representation of it
in feminine 4m,
in my eyes, she like the sky
covers me
com4tably, angelically
this woman, my savior,
a canopy that shields me from danger
                    -- calms my anger
i am the world below her
like geb and nut without the separation
instead, we have a rah union
blooming in each others' sight

at least ... i'm smiling

darker than earth tone flesh
dressed in a green
warrior's gown
her hair a spherical crown
around her waste a yellow belt
a sword at her side
the wind gently rides under her

i rest on a bed in a red room
i thank her 4 saving me
my wordz barely audible
she smiles
i tell her my name iz maa kheru
true of voice,
voice of truth

but she tells me i am destiny
last son of the 1s they call father aquarius
and mother pisces
bruthaz b strong and hero
our clan the multiple zero
in pale king's equation

destined 2 reduce the pale king 2 nothing

i tell her,
"father aquarius has died
mother pisces' mind iz paralyzed
as my clan lies set on assimilating
                    -- with the pale king
a dangerous descision
the pale king's vision
iz 2 police our thoughts,
control them
his plan iz not 1 of freedom."

the woman says,
"my name iz Dess,
half of God
but no less
i am the daughter
of the queen haj-va-rah
the descendant of God
i am daughter of the queen mother
the earth respects her hour
as i am heir 2 her power
i am God's courier,
feminine warrior
when ideals fall 2 far right
we defend what's left
and your grief i have felt
i know my mother will provide u help."

"where am i?"

"u r in the kammasi kingdom
we prepare 4 revolution
we have attacked the pale king
            -- from the other side of this war
we battle under auset
matriarch, descendant
it iz the queen that iz chosen
and the daughter that receives the inheritance

the king iz the general of the army
protectors of the garden we cultivate
we have culture 2 satiate, feed u knowledge
wordz of wisdom that even u could learn from
with all your lessons, beautiful sun."

my lips move slowly,
floating,
like in a dream
"i must see the queen."

"in presence"

haj-va-rah
queen of God
adorned with light
born from night
her spirit's height extends
          -- 2 the heavens
she rests in an ivory chair
wears a diadem of locked hair
cloaked in a gown
the colour of the sky
she sits beside the king
his hair shaven,
he iz dressed in gold armor,
he holds a sword in his right hand
his left hand empty
windstaff strapped 2 the back
                    -- of his onyx throne
power honed thru wordz,
magic conjured from queen's and king's lips
they kiss the air every time they speak
and as i reach their throne
i bow at their feet

it iz them
descendants
genesis
2 revelations
and all books in between

numbers
psalms
acts
samuel ii
ezekiel
isaiah
jeremiah
amos

the king tosses his sword
it lands be4 me,
the queen stands and asks
"what brings u 2 our land?"

"i am the hero"

i recount the stories
the losses
the glory
the future concern
the worries
i recount our adventures
            -- in wide areas
the death of father aquarius
the death of the shogun,
his redemption,
i tell them my clan iz in disarray
i tell them we have come at a cross
the end of days
and then i let my wordz dance
i tell them who i am
maa kheru
true of voice
voice of truth
it's cryptic
but i speak:

"my queen, my king
i am the hero u seek
the page with the proverb
            -- written in ink
i am the knight of pens
your daughter was destined 2 meet
i am blessed with the spell
slipped from my lips
2 plant upon the queen
and wake her from her sleep
revive her in the rays of her son

in law, i am the sun that guides u
            -- by light and prophetic dreams
who makes love 2 your moon-daughter singer
i am the magic and air between your fingers
i am the warrior ready 2 protect u when u r in need

the clean and holy water u drink from God's stream
i am the tears of joy that u weep
i am the mystical chant that u must speak
the wish/prayer/secret u need 2 keep
i am the wheel of 4tune
and i stand at the peek of the pyramids
          -- that africans built in 3840 plus genius weeks
i am that 7th wonder that still holds u hypnotized
constructed when the dawn first opened its eyes,
but now those eyes cry,
its chosen people have lost the feast
the fruit of knowledge
          -- God truthfully allowed them to eat
but do not worry
i am that hero u seek

i am the strength that lies inside u
the temperance and force that binds u
i am the world at your feet
the love between the couple u greet
the joy in the dancers who sing 2 the beat
i am the flow in the breeze and air,
the last of those who care
the armor u wear
the cross that u bare
the warning visions/enchantments
          -- that surfaces from the deep
i am the star that lights the path
2 the sentry that will grant u entry
and give u the weapon of the staff
2 battle the man with more than half the answers
i am the man who grips love in his hands
the 1 who will save the land
and let the flowers grow from the ground
--pulled up from all the way down--
i am the thief who steals the puzzle of war
and leaves u with just a peace
my queen
my king
i am the hero u seek."

"they ceremony"

with gold plates
and silver utensils
adorned with
roast meat
chicken grease,
broccoli rice and shrimp
dressing,
sprinkled with seasoned salt
cut corn, candied yams
cranberry fruit sauce
chalices filled with stardust
a li'l sunbeam seasoning the gravy
wavy crescent rolls and breadsticks
pumpkin and apple pie,
sweet potato on the side
white cake with sweet frost
          we begin a feast of queens and kings

in this bright place
we got BOOM BANDZ playing
the queen praising peace
while during the feast
          -- her daughter dess
teaches me 2 eat properly
cuz the warrior in me
got a monopoly
i b rugged scoundrel
i tell her,
"i'm not always like this
it's just that life's whip
has scratched my back,
revenge has taken me back
trapped in savage emotions
and my thoughts r on my clan
hoping ancestor spirits
          -- and my prayers watch over them."

dess takes my hand

guides me from my seat
and leads me in2 a dance
slow
eyes closed
we grow in2 1 another
she asks me who i am
and i tell her,
"son 2 father and mother
brother 2 hero and strong
enemy 2 my enemies.
who am i 2 u?"

"maa kheru," she answers. "that iz truth."

i slip from her arms
creep from the room
and wander in2 the dark
night dawned ...
my thoughts rise in2 the sky
they hold a conversation
           -- with the stars
none can find aquarius
pisces has become dim
no sword in my hand
i ask,
"how can i find revenge?"

"first, come 2 your senses,"
           -- i heard dess speak behind me
"revenge iz not what u seek.
it iz love and peace;
u r love and i am your peace.
our signs r a match."

"ancestral symmetry"

she said our signs were a match
so, i struck a conversation
but her feminine inspiration
          -- swirled in2 the heavens
she discussed our future in council
she told the stars she would change the ways
          -- of this rugged scoundrel
she told me,
"in order 2 open your book
i have 2 break the seal 2 your heart."
that's where the heavens told her 2 start
she told me my life was art and that it was priceless
she said,

"any earthly crisis
could b deflected
by all astronomical devices
          -- your father aquarius
          -- your mother pisces."

she my wife,
the 4m of isis
it was her mystical 4m
that told me 2 write this
yes, dess existed as inspiration
she was my interest when she had no 4m
but still the brightest

and her star gave me direction
          -- when there was no map, guidance or tactic
and now i vow 2 hold her up
cuz she iz my world,
and i am atlas

her smile clean and phat
and i spell that with a 'ph'
becuz she brings balance 2 my life
and 2 the 'ph' i add a 'd'

4 the 360 d-grees i rotate around her
she may b this kingdom's daughter,
but i revolve around her
becuz she iz the sun

intellectually bright
her soul? nurturing
and her body? hot
i scorch my tongue
when i kiss her sunspot
taste her nubian juice
trained as love's new recruit

inside her mahogany pyramid-temple
my wordz will recycle
thru 800,000,000
potential innocent children
who grow from her as disciples
climax in a big bang and BOOM!
create room in our universe
            -- of infinite stars, planets, & moons
            -- grown in her womb

our children,
gods and goddesses
of every heavenly body
invited at birth
united by verse
u'n'i verse
anything that wishes our children harm

that's what we r 2gether
what r u separate?

"who i am"

she smiled
and spoke
her voice
a deep melody

"i am genesis
the genes-of-isis
i preceded all chronometrical devices
becuz i am the beginning of time
the 1st tick and tock of God's mind
so, do u know who i am?
i am a black woman,
african
it was me who stood 1st
        -- in God's land
when i cried
my tears divided
and created man

molded from the sands
i am from the earth
my breast leaked love 1st
then mixed with milk, honey and tears
and became the foundation of the 1st church

the black man drank my wordz
called them scripture
that i delivered as pslams
and quenched him of his thirst

i sang in sync
with nature's beat
and created language
that u still speak
in your verse

my body produces gold, silver,
diamonds, and a pearl u call life

i am morning and night
it was thru my power and reason
that nature split in2 4 seasons
i was worshipped, revered,
and idolized by individuals, families,
            -- and nations
i am the mother of civilization
i have been queen,
goddess,
diplomat,
scientist,
icon,
scholar,
prophet,
and freedom fighter
i held jesus in my arms
when his name was heru
i tell u i am nefertari
'God's wife of amen'
'the beautiful companion'
i defied death,
resurrected as queen istnofret
defying death, i was deified in life
defended my people from strife

i was makeda, they called sheba
dahia al-kahina, defender of freedom
pushed barbarians away from my kingdom
burned my land in resistance
and God 4give my decision
when i chose 2 spare my children,
my babies,
so that they could escape slavery
their bodies dying
but their spirits rising 2wards heaven

i have been lynched, burned, beaten, branded
left stranded on a land i was forced 2 re-mold
i was sold like cattle
battled a war on the inside as well as out

my image has been abused
but my spirit has refused defeat
my rope 2 God iz no noose
it iz the voice i use 2 sing
i can bring u 2 your knees
            -- when i chant the blues

i've even taught u
            -- maa kheru --
a thing or 2
thru your mother's voice
every time i speak, i sing
i harmonize nature with my voice
and u have no choice but 2 love me again
african-black woman,
i'm beyond super-human

my beauty eclipses the sun's rays
has immortals dying young and kings enslaved
and all the gods bow 2wards me 4 praise
i am the 21 year reign of hatshepsut
i am the tiye that binds
i am love's 3rd eye
'fiery eye of rah'
the warrior-queen nzingha

so who r u,
maa kheru
(besides truth)?"

i answer,
"black knight 2 black queen
i am your checkmate, maa kheru
the fight 2 secure your image --- iz the war i fight 4 u."

"wind & earth"

the taste of revenge dissolves
dess's kiss sweetens my lips
and i fall 2 my knees,
i hug her waist
and kiss her on the space
where new life breathes
her dress lifts by a magical breeze
and my lips r free 2 kiss her entire body
my clothes r shed,
like skins and past labors

our bodies rub against 1 another
smooth, cottony, like 2 clouds
          -- gliding and becoming 1
without friction
and we r sipping,
lightly tickling with kiss
          -- and finger tips
we drip soul on2 each other's body
and we love in waves,
crashing on2 each others' shores
and my sword iz no longer a weapon
but a tool 4 affection
standing straight, erection
as she keeps pressing up against it
          -- with lips and hips
and i hold on2 her,
becuz she iz all i've got
here in the spotlight of the moon
nature watching,
the great voyeur
the grass growing beneath my back,
and beneath hers
as we merge
our hearts can b heard
beating, increasing
speaking in wordz of another language

she releases me from anguish
gives me the world
as i dive 2 retrieve her pearl
my seeds swirl deep in her earth

she and i become W.E.
and we split,
switch positions
her the Wind
i the Earth's harp
and she blows,
plays licks on my strings
and 2gether we flow

time takes a minute 4 itself
as dess and i grow in2 each other's bodies
my back arched,
howling at the moon,
myself deep in dess's tomb
where life iz buried
her heart tugging on my heart
i part with my soul
and throw it in2 her, the center

my holy ghost floats
i dangle from a metaphysical rope
connecting me 2 my physical body
i fill dess's space
and feel her body quake
pour lakes that inundate destiny and fate
i can now trace the footsteps and paths
          -- our children will walk in

dess iz talking in quick breaths
and my body rolls like thunder over her
my spirit leaps back in2 the physical plane
my energy in her, her energy in me
and we r still drained
we remain chained 2 each others' frame
without friction,
but we still have a flame
here as we go
gone as we came

"kheru's eye"

the sun's eye
peeks over
the horizon

dess glides on the wind
and takes her place
at the window
she says,
"let us show the sun
how we glow when we mold."

and i crawl on my hands and soul
so low, i divide, liquefy and flow
my body drips and pours
i become a tide on the floor
my crawl iz a wave
and i solidify
2 embrace and taste her space
our bodies in nep-tuned with 1 another
i put my tongue on venus
and eclipse mars
every star wishing they were our son
her breath pounds the air like a drum
her heavenly body jumps
my tongue shapes poems i wrote 4 her
private poetry
just between her and me
something only she can read
and the sun can relate
dess's breath breaks

jazz is played
as she presses her lips
against my instrument
and i quiver,
shiver
from warmth

we become adorned
with each other's body
she faces the sun
and i run kisses down her spine
back up 2 her neck
inhale her breath

she kisses a cross on my back
on my stomach,
in my lap
and my handz twist her naps
until she iz locked
in that spot called 'there'
her hair now a flare

up in the sky,
the sun's eye iz fully aware
the 2 of us bare our souls
and wish the sun can grow from us
with daughters, like water
2 flow
2 flow
2 flow

"arming of the heru"

it started physically
placed on my body
was a black cloak
soaked in earth's oil
anointed by the sky's soil

haj-va-rah sprinkled royal stardust
that locked up
and as it dried
it divided in2 matter,
that turned in2 silver and gold
          -- as the wind roared
and 4med a sword on the floor

then came spring,
summer, fall, and winter
the seasons came 2gether,
4med letters,
blended every raging weather element
swirling until it became vapor
nature reversing time,
scattering in2 paper
with wordz scribed
          -- by a metaphysical-ink particle
4ming the articles
          -- that r this kingdom's lessons
now my mind's weapon

a chorus of prayers/chants
made my soul dance,
cool as the autumn breeze
flowing like the sea
mind, spirit, and body
all as 1
no longer a divide
i will return 2 my clan --- revived

warrior-queen at my side

Act V: The Journey Up

"2 my clan"

as we step,
we blend
transparent
there iz e-mergence
on time's current
we skip,
and dance
our 4ms so blurred,
hip-notic
we leave nature in a trance

sending messages
across great distances
i contact jamaal,
sha-nun,
and rufus
our minds linked
sinking in2 a silent,
and invisible conversation,

i ask
in a telepathic breath,
"what's happened
since i've left?"

"mother pisces
iz still,
unconscious
brother hero and strong
meditate inside the vibe of language
sitting atop a word
humming supreme mathematics
counting the days
when they can plan a raid
teamed with the sun's rays
against the pale king's haze

they plan in ways

and search 4 allies
with powers and vibes
2 save our clan, our tribe
our ancient,
spiritual pride

our eyes can see the final hour
when spirits shower on us
we will bathe in yesterday's presence
our past lessons secured in the future
this iz our time 2 act -- attack

it's dangerous
that d'win controls our secrets
but he hasn't spoken them yet
we must cut him from his breath
our less-Sons and Daughters must b protected
and become more than the warriors this world has made us
d'win has become injustice."

"no.
we will strike
where the problem lies
we will summon allies
from our collective and others

their lives their tithe
jamaal,
sha-nun,
rufus,
when next we attack,
the pale king dies."

"we summon"

we journey
2 the word
drums pounding
calling us

we look up
at the bass
we see space
cosmo canyon
rising in2 heaven

drums summon
our presence
we don't climb,
          -- we rise

and as our eyes
come in focus
we see a band
of rebel poets

cousins in our struggle
lead by a man named torio
warrior of pen and fist
descendant of the righteous
heirs 2 the land we fight in

we have not been
the only 1s summoned
rebel poets
come from
the quezacotl temple
their wordz plural,
not single
bilingual

our wordz pumping,
thundering with the drum

we ra unite
strong and hero
mother pisces,
she laying still

>>and we summon<<

we summon our spirits
summoned from the heavens
our bodies ascend
blend in2 the night

up in2 the sky,
out in2 space
we trace
astronomical movements

we open our mouths
and inhale space
our lips laced with the sun

around us,
the stars gather
become a mass of energetic matter
building as we float
filling our throats

we r soaring,
heaven's bodies roaring
surrounded
by a violet aura

i put the fury
of zach de la rocha's voice
          -- on my spine
2 hold me up
tom morello's sonic sound
tim bob's bass pounds
and my heart becomes

-- wilk's kick drum --

our natural elements begin rockin' with rahkim
so naturally we become mic-RAH-phone fiendz
as we rage against this machine

we have the current of cain
and the blood of able
the knights of the periodic table
we matter
let this dragon's 10 horns shatter
stop it from blowing off key notes
rumbling fire in its throat
let us descend 2 battle him
and all his demonic inharmonic children
with our own beautiful hymns
poetry rumbling the word
in phat verses made up of lines so thin
between righteousness and their sins

so, we descend
our spirits,
our powers
summoned

bald heads
imbibe the sun
locks become
electric strands
weapons in hand,
and in mind
we have found
our time

and with this word,
we must stand firm --- and attack

"from the word"

nature iz not right
dess has left
fled in2 the night

it iz now morning
the sun giving us warning
the biting aura of war swarming
our powers warming our bodies

but, we don't ceremony ...
we don't dance ...
we r 5% of our clan

our shadow lightened
and our syllables muted ---
our wordz banned
clan disbanded
our music silenced
no rhythm or sound from band
atop this syllabic stage
surrounded by thought police
led by tag
coupled with d'win
and cold stares from our clan

tag's voice ascends,
"u can b pardoned
4 your sins
your crimes can b 4gotten.

we have come 4 your assistants
2 help the pale king
put down another clan's resistance
the 36 staten fiendz.

your reward,
freedom
and between us, peace

we can even release
        -- mother pisces from sleep."

i stare in2 tag's eyes
hoping he would cry what i feel
but he has no emotions
what little soul he has
keeps groping my thoughts
he captures them

but i feel the breeze
the cool, the wind
and i whisper,
"we'll handle him."

brother strong and hero at my side
the only ally iz jamaal
rufus,
sha-nun,
they split,
leading a small group
ready 4 action

the rebel poet faction,
ready at arms

i see dust on the horizon

i speak clearly 2 tag,
"u just don't know
where u've walked
u've talked so long
your own song,
out of tune,
has become a smooth,
and looped melody

so let me explain it 2 u
in your own loop,
and in ours,

u have been caught
and ...
u just don't know
where u've walked."

tag asks,
"and where iz that?"

"u and your thought police
have just walked in2 a trap."

the dust becomes soldiers
pouring on2 the land
dess out in front,
her mother's army
at her command

torio and his rebel poets
flow with the east wind
they descend on the thought police
descend deep,
their spirits awakened from sleep
tossing off passive shackles,
it iz now time 4 action and battle

our clan, once seduced
have been lifted from the ruse
the offbeat loop
of the pale king's false dream
battle cries and screams
they tear at the thought police's seams

tag's massive army on the defense
d'win drops 2 his knees 2 repent
brothers, ally, and i
glide thru shadows
and strike from the heart of the word
the 1st of 4 lessons
the word, the most powerful of weapons
loud enough 2 silence wars

tied 2 God and Goddess by vocal chords
4med with our soul
and tempering an ancestral sword

the battle parts in 2

tag screams,
"u will die!"

"i will not die on your time
but on my terms
and i'll return
resurrected by lessons learned
2 battle u."

tag comes in2 view,
"don't think
your queen
will escape fate
she will b raped by my hands
much like this land
i'll shatter every1 of your crystal thoughts
back in2 sand

and i'll burn your spirit
your soul,
your holy ghost
wrap them up on my page
as if they were the wordz i wrote
the verses i spoke
i'll place your soul 2 my lips
so that the ashes can b smoked."

"u'd choke,
inhaling me
the poet-tency
of my poetry
cuz the only thing i smoke,
is competition
with the wordz written

in my lessons and compositions
it's like these griots
tearing thru your opposition
i'll warn u now 2 use your intuition
cuz u know it would b foolish
2 go thru with this
up against the rudest,
crudest,
ruthless,
hectic,
kemetic knights
whose methods r so powerful
they gave birth 2,
and killed your whole style,
then resurrected it

like jesus of nazareth did lazarus
like the sun said 2 the fool
be4 he stepped from the cliff
and took his last breath,
'your folly iz most curious,
have u no fear of death?'

cuz even while your style
starved 4 knowledge
i fed it
cursed the air
where your wordz were birthed
and then blessed it
with my own,
voice in perfect tone
(2 heal the wretched)
while i covered up your crimes
and in the same rhyme and line
made u confess 2 it.

burned u at the stake
like a jesuit heretic
and that's the real trick
now isn't?

so get back, tag
my wordz r sick
u may catch the pro-verb-i-all flu
but i'm not worried about that
cuz i'm as far beyond knowledge/time
as knowledge/time r beyond u."

we r back in dance
battling, like the battle
of the in-town chant
tag defends
with the double-blade lance

brothers, ally, and i
swinging windstaffs,
swordz,
and battle cries

weapons fly,
flash, clash
voices crash
guns clap
earth's field
iz battle mass

i take a step,
skip, twirl
my sword cuts
and slash
tag's lance
splits in half

brothers hero and strong
take my place,
slashing at tag
he defends
with lance in either hand

tag exhales,
"i've learned this much

take what u can,
when u can."

"then,
u've
learned
nothing."[7]

i attack,
thrusting

the blow iz blocked,
i'm tossed away
i jump 2 my feet
and slay two thought police

i watch
jamaal and tag
they battle
the earth rumbles
and rattles, it screams

the ground iz bleeding
blood distorts natural colour
clusters of bodies piled 2 heaven
and this iz hell on earth

whether jail or church
i must pray
my mother's and father's spirits
cover our swords' blades
faith iz restored
shimmering in my mind, body, soul
and on my sword

i am the reflection of this glow
i calm my thoughts,

---

[7] quote from "The Secret of Nihm"

let them grow
from the lessons i've learned
it heals the scars i've earned

i am clear as air
clean as can b
while spirits
shower and drip over me

brothers strong and hero
jump back 2 tag
each thrust and blow,
sword swing, and flow
push tag back

tag makes fatal move
and a sword
is thrust thru
either shoulder

tag drops his weapons
his blood flowing
dripping in2 his hands
his breath,
few

he speaks,
"my body will dissolve
eaten by the earth
but i will birth new hatred
my presence,
my spirit,
will never die."

my sword
tears thru
tag's heart

"that will b
4 my future children 2 decide."

the bodies of the thought police
            -- glow
melt like snow
and disappear

out there,
the pale king
sits scared

and he should b
becuz we will come
4 him

"we celebrate"

past the gates
of haj-va-rah's palace
we celebrate
and praise God

we ra unite with clan
d'win repents,
his hands 2gether
we console him
with spirit and rhythm
he knows 4giveness
will come from the journey
of his own spirit

i introduce dess
2 the rest of my clan,
close friends and allies
we vibe on the songs
from brother strong
as he anoints the mic

we dance,
surrounded by night
cousins 2 stars
called fireflies
we cry in each other's arms

mother pisces
can now see
she awakened
by our aquarian father

his spirit hollers loud
that he has never been
more proud of his sons

we have become
the image of our parents

and it will never b shattered

our feet
scitter
scatter
dancing
on the floor
we celebrate
our days
our nights
our 4evers --- all in a future past this war

"separated by birth"

sweetly,
dess speaks

she tells me
that she lays down
          -- her sword
becuz inside her
iz our life

i tell her
that i must descend
leave,
become a legend
and return 2 her
as her man,
and as life's father

"out there,
the pale king trembles
counting plural days
down 2 single

and he iz all that remains
4 us 2 change our present,
secure our future,
and innerstand our past

our paths will cross and clash
but i will return back 2 this spot
i will not die

i will live beyond and far
past the age of stars
that our eyes
have just focused on

in absence
i will b a legend.
just a word spoken
            -- by your lips
just half of a kiss

but i will return ..."

"the last stanza"

this iz how i became a legend

i see thru a single 'i'
master poet samurai
descendant of the khemi
servant 2 the clan gemini
led by an aquarian resolution
and the tears pisces cried

with strong and hero,
my pen/sword against paper glide
rufus and sha-nun my only guides
with jamaal at my side

un4tunately made ronin
when the stars against me aligned
cancer infected aquarius
and put out the constellation's light
wordz dripped on2 paper from my eyes bright

now i wander the countryside
pen/sword as my only way 2 survive
disenfranchised griot-samurai
wandering against my will
working odd jobs with my skills
hired 2 kill
take down others' competition 4 a simple meal
and a little money 2 carry me 2 the next deal

i upped my fees
when my reputation spread like a disease
            -- and wildfire
i was feared, envied, and admired
my name a 2nd language in people's mouths
and in their breath my name found a home
but i still roam

i step in2 kingdoms

like the nameless gun-totting mariachi
with weapons in my pack
containing more power
than what destroyed nagasaki
and the knowledge of 5 scrolls
scribed by the ronin samurai miyamoto musashi

my style cannot b copied or imitated
my enemies become intimidated
as my eyes change colours with my mood
like the leaves change colours with the seasons
the ink in my pen the same way

emotions up
i can't fail
shadow covers my face
like the minister's black veil
lights dim just 4 me
like the mysterious hero
in an ancient tale

and i keep my mind clear of smoke
against my enemies it's murder i wrote
cuz their think tank iz broke and leaking
my words r heat seeking grooves
the strength of a thousand heroes in 1 syllable
and the power of a thousand stampeding shires' hooves

my next move iz 2 the stage
my enemies' next move iz 2 the grave
when my wordz rush and drown them in a flood
their pride bruised without ointment on it 2 rub

my competition doesn't understand
            -- a certain samurai proverb
            -- which iz stated as such:
            "in order 4 a samurai 2 b the most brave
            they must have at least a drop of african blood"

and my heritage inundates on2 the page

enemies get burned with only 1 heated gaze
                    -- instantly slayed
when my power overflows like the nile
i drop my pen and defeat my enemies freestyle

a legend born at the road's end
but again i begin
i paved a new road less traveled
my backpack contains all the artifacts
from the tower of babel
once again the pen i grapple
setup a secret poetry chapel

i become a rhythm on the run
and a beat hard 2 catch
my pen cuts me loose from my enemies' nets
the pale king finds me a threat
he wants 2 make me his next victim
makin' it hard 4 me 2 go near any civilized system
but a challenge like that i only make it my mission
2 send my adversaries 6 feet deep
and their families with them
they die knee deep
in the poor rhetoric of their own children
              -- from my pen

that's my bushido flow
the path of the griot-warrior
            -- the way i go
4med by dioxirhybo - nucleic acid trip
i throw an infinite amount of sharp lines
and throwing stars
in the shape of parentheses and brackets
my style u can't trap it -- track it
if u shout a threat then back it

my name whispered all at once
causes ruckuses and rackets
i attack in the active and the passive
make 135 lbs seem massive

the strength of my wordz
can't even b calculated in scientific notation
i'm lookin' 4 whoever's next
in the high magistrate's rotation

take down the pale king's nation
            -- my invasion
no trade on my vocation
it's got me jailed without probation
with my poems and slogans
coupled with the voice i sing
this poet ronin iz out 2 slay the pale king

that evil man
who tried 2 hire me
2 take out the 36-staten clan
and their highest officials
and steal their manual
that reveals the secret
of their intellectual, lyrical rituals

instead,
the staten clan and i
planned 2 take the pale king's head
and the 14 scrolls and 10 manuals
hidden underneath his bed

up north i fled
with a ticket 2 visit the empire nation
and temple done anew
with the artistic view
the griot, outercollective ally, kung fu
over 1000 styles
none outdone by a number even close 2 few

and so i recruit the 4 samurai
with the attitudes that'll wreckya
deckya,
lyrically --- but seriously ---

if the pale king really wanted a test
we'd have 2 do it 2 him physically

maniacally like #1, the protector
instru--mentally like #2, the emancipator
(don't mess with him
he wears a red dragon diadem
under shaolin discipline)
just as dangerously as #3, the judge
aka: the educator, the g-laser,
shock u like a taser
or #4, wahr,
lyrically set 4 stun
like an electron phaser

like david or akenenaten's psalms
comin' down upon the pale king
with more wrath than khan
with prophetic revelations deeper than john

this crew iz 2 bad 2 b known as heroes
2 good 2 b known as criminals
verse mercenaries -- my adversaries' adversaries
on the average, this crew iz mean
professional like golgo 13
armed with liquid swordz, lightsabers,
windstaffs and fatal flying guillotines
plus we were teamed with the 36 staten fiends

the pale king fired his unholy magical beams
we counter attacked with a balance
and phoenix downed our inner talents
stormed the castle
and easily cut thru the pale king's crew
hittin' the competition so quick and fast
it looked like we had more arms
than that indian god vishnu

lit them up with the power of the god ramuh
and the original trinity of kemet

ausar, heru, and auset
they were hit by our 41st fleet
no time 2 retreat -- accept defeat
they had no chance except the chants 2 their false god

but his head lay in my left hand
and in my right, his weapon, the wand
down were the walls
of this pale king's facade
shattered by this holy-griot mob
(with stolen manuals and scrolls)

afterwards,
we split in2 our respected crews
36 statens, 4 samurai
and i

1 ronin who keeps roamin'
without master 2 serve and b indentured
forced 2 the road,
and wander
in search of an all new adventure

"journey continued"

i return 2 dess's arms
her body 4 months
filled with life
i recount how the pale king's
        -- strife had ended

we blend and merge
in2 a circle of friends,
families and allies
and i pray,

"father,
triple eye
guide my tribe
under the divide of day
play the night's song
as the moon rises in the sky
nature's nocturnal vibe
it cries the sun's light

we r the 1st children of the sun
we r the melanin drops
        -- that fade in2 the night
        -- and absorb the day
every ray of the sun iz dedicated 2 us
we r focused on our scribe religion
2 give this rough cut world
a new revision

our mission,
2 marry nature
and dance
2 her beat
sacrifice every tree
burn in magical vapors
make paper 2 scribe spells
and savor our creative labor

magical minute record breakers
span past time's barriers
message carriers
2 children unseen
our seeds
from Mother Earth
birth a future generation
where our scribble/scrabbled wordz
will b deciphered 4 their imaginations."

so,
let the sun rise high
as we all ra unite
4 inner
and outer--
collective allies alike
(peace)

Extra Worx by Teferu Azr

Extra Worx

"Composure"

who's that,
with the sensual appeal?
beautiful **BLACK** woman
come 4th and let me tell u how i feel
that u look good enough 2 compose
whether in instrumental musical song notes
lyrical poems or paragraph prose
lord knows your image helps my words flow
either sung from my lips
or conjured from the papermate wand at my finger tips
down 2 and scribed on2 this ancient african papyrus
there's a simple mathematical 4mula 4 this
all the variables that make up your equation
           equals the solution 2 my loneliness
the 2 of us as 1 = holiness
but the challenge is
4 words 2 compare 2 this
           -- more or less --
describe what god made flesh
and leave everyone in awe and impressed
as i address the reason why jesus wept
           -- your beauty --
a secret god has kept from His lips
now told thru mine
with words so magical they can turn water in2 wine
and in your honor hold back the sands and winds of time
2 never effect your beauty natural and incalculable
and give description 2 what has become my sensual and
central addiction
a luscious taste of feminine beauty beyond human
comprehension
but please allow me 2 bring it 2 this earthly dimension
starting with the allure of your hair
which snakes down in spiraling curls, twirls
or tightened strands of wool
pulled over my eyes like lies
but this b the truth
u, god's proof that there r angels

Extra Worx

hair tightened up and tangled
hangin' low or up in that silk african wrap
or underneath gold, bronze, or onyx crown
which becomes undone
melted in the sun
and poured down upon your body's skin
like spirits enlightened
causing more BOOMS! in my heart
than the clash of the titans
whether light or dark
dark or light
african woman, u brighten my life
4med by god's thought light, spirit, and dream
in2 the perfect woman being
why try the carbon copy
when none compares 2 the original queen

and although clouds try 2 hide u
your light always shines thru
and my lips always find u
2 kiss your belly when life grows inside u
in many shades of the earth soil god has painted u
the devil has tried tainting u
1 day this knight will b rewarded 4 saving u
until then, i apologize,
cuz even with all the power in my pen,
"i can only protect u ... i can't fight a war 4 u."[8]
so i wrap my arms around u in protection
a little affection
this holy confession
like my tongue caressing
      -- your holy blessing
fulfilling all of my wishes
chocolate princess
the only way 2 describe u is: spiritually delicious

---

[8] line from Star Wars Episode I: The Phantom Menace

Extra Worx

"i dance" (in the memory of amadou diallo)

i dance by thunder's vibe
unnatural fire flies
dancing in my eyes
as my spirit joins me
                    -- by my side

i hear the pound of offbeat drums
the heat of an unnatural sun
runs thru me
and i dance -- thunder chants
and clouds of smoke become ghosts
echoing these past dance steps
i dance 2 the west
in the direction of sun-goes-down
past spirits resurrected from the ground

past sounds echoed in the present
our gift, time shifts permanently
4ever will it b, 2 speak
as i dance
            -- with those who just walk the beat
who seek me out 4 their dance partner
their tears, their armor
but they rain on me
shower on me
cold weather
without warning of 'freeze'
but the rain has me in a trance
i dance

my arms and legs wild
i waltz and tap with my feet
my fate in synch with the beat
i dance 2 their tune
only becuz i look like me
physically prepared 2 dance
                    -- on their command
and my image, shattered

Extra Worx

lingers in the sands of time
and crime iz defined by the sign
        -- that tells me i don't belong here

here where the anchors dropped
the middle passage stopped
and the mentality
of history's longevity docked
the cargo locked in chains

here i remain
stained with thoughts
caught uptempo
every rhythm on the repeat
i rotate 360 degrees
but that's okay
cuz bruthaz and sistaz
        -- r always talkin' 'bout revolution
and here we r
revolving back 2 the start
the foundation on which this nation lies
at least my revolution was televised

i b a poor man
peddling truth
dancing 2 loops
        -- of liars
lyres playing songs
of premature
dawns
cackling fires
that substitute 4 the sun
leaving mother and father empty
but do not worry
my dance has made me holy
19 times

and the beat rushes thru my veins
my eyes rolling back 2 the past
and i see things haven't changed

Extra Worx

i died back then
just the same
under different names
different laws,
different rights,
my name was once christ

crucified by bloodtype
my type of blood
runs 2 remind u
that time rewinds u
binds u 2 the ways
of their laws
on this stole-land
and so i dance on the 1
black history made this month

dancing 2 41 claps
but i only catch 19 beats
on these streets
ruled by martial law walkers
new york--texas rangers
crossing ash bridges
dancing with me
4 me 2 b touched by an angel
and if u missed the ball
u can read all about it
　　　　-- in the early edition

my rendition
of the repetition
of history's dance
we have been van damned
kicked around
pound 4 pound
sold 4 soul
i roll with their thunder
and i wonder why these hunters
have gathered me 2 their ceremony

Extra Worx

and only bruthaz and sistaz
and cousins have thought about it
that a loaded wallet in the handz
        -- of a black man iz dangerous anyway
and, so i dance
2 masturbating hearts
their thoughts ejaculating fog
and that iz how they got off
and my spirit stands still
and still i stand in the past
asking as i extend my handz,
                    "may i have this dance?"

Lectures-In-Rhyme

<u>The Soul of Mythology</u>: Teferu Azr gives an in-depth look at the driving force of all mythology and religion. The Black Divine, or the Divinity of Blackness runs subtly through the rhythms of language, song, and definitely the mythologies of all cultures and the top four religions of Islam, Christianity, Judaism, and Hinduism. At the heart of every true myth is the desire/innerstanding to being Black. Heroes are the divine process of dark matter, dark energy, and melanin. Villains are the representation of the mysteries of Blackness. Teferu Azr explores this as well as other phenomenon of myth, religions, and legends. He exposes how the writers of modern day myths are continuing this tradition; and he also exposes how and why many Black writers have lost this sense of knowledge, wisdom, and innerstanding.

<u>The Medusa Complex</u>: A lecture about how European Society took what was valued and sacred to the Ancient Black People and reversed the concepts into diabolical configurations for the masses to fear, especially Black People themselves. Once afraid of the bastardized concepts, Black People would then never explore how these

concepts empowered them, came from them, and held a beautiful and extremely spiritual connotation. Teferu Azr speaks on all that is presented as evil is actually a foundation of creation and Ancient Black Power. From the character of 'Medusa' to even the word "Nigger", their origins are divine, misunderstood, and purposely misconstrued.

Computer Blues: The Masonic DNA Imperative: A lecture on how the design of technology mirrors the design of the soul. But, what is the missing ingredient to the technological and synthetic?

Matriarch vs. Patriarch: Teferu Azr explores the concept of the two systems and reveals how they first started off in unity and how they have been dissected from one another and the origin of the destruction of a unified Mother and Father state.

The Paradigm of the Hero: A continuation of 'The Soul of Mythology' lecture, this takes up with the path of the hero and where many modern day myths and Black writers fail to make the connection with who the Hero is and what must be done to attain balance.

Cultural Schizophrenia and the Wish Master Named Melanin: A look into Western Civilizations destruction of unfied concepts and its link to the story of Aladdin and the Lamp.

PLUS:

Hollow Daze

Sexual Melanin: The Hero's Addiction 2 The Heroine

The Fool's Errand

Artistic Alchemy

For Information on the purchase of these lectures, or for Teferu Azr to present them visit the website www.dachosen.com.

Plus, available soon, the companion book to the Lecture In Rhyme Series, The Black Divine Science Vol. I.

Coming Soon…

From Mis-Edu-Caged 2 Knowledge Born

From a Prison of Mist 2 a City of The Sun

From Slave 2 General

From a Silent Battle 2 a Spoken War

The Legacy of Kahm Noiz Chronicles a battle 4
the Ances-Tree and all its leaves

The Ungodz vs. The Enlightened G.O.D.Z.

The 2nd Epic Poem by Teferu Azr

"2 Enlighten The G.O.D.Z."

Suggested Reading

Nile Valley Contributions to Civilization
   By Anthony Browder
Blacked Out Through Whitewash
   By Dr. Suzar Epps
The Golden Age of the Moors
   Edited by Ivan Van Sertima
Daghetto Tymz (subscribe at daghettotymz.com)

The Isis Papers
   By Dr. Francis Cress Welsing
Books by Gerald Massey
Books by John Henrik Clarke
Books by Dr. Yosef ben-Jochannan
The Lost Books of the Bible
The Medu Neter Vol 1 & 2
   By Ra Un Nefer Amen
The Hidden History of D.C.
The Hidden History of New York
The Hidden History of Boston
   By Tingba Apidta
The Bahavagita
The Rig Veda
The Mahabarata
The Epic of Gilgamesh